ABBREVIATIO

UNIT CODE

second Company, sixth Battalion, Royal Artillery (2C6B)
sixth/tenth Battalion, Royal Artillery (6-10B)
eighth Company, tenth Battalion, Royal Artillery (8C10B)
first Battery, first Brigade, Royal Artillery (1B1B)
first Battery, fourth Brigade, Royal Artillery (1B4B)
seventh Battery, second Brigade, Royal Artillery
(7B2B) first Battery, fifteenth Brigade, Royal
Artillery (1B15B)
first Marines (New South Wales and Norfolk Island) (1M)
second Marines (Port Phillip (Melbourne) and Van Diemensland) (2M)
third Marines (Fort Essington) (3M)
fourth Marines (Sydney and Hobart) (4M)
Royal Marines Light Infantry (Cape York) (RMLI) Border
Police (BP)
1/third East Kent (The Buffs) Regiment of Foot (3)
1/fourth Kings Own Regiment of Foot (4)
1/fifth Northumberland Fusiliers (5)
1/eleventh North Devonshire Regiment of Foot (11)
1/twelfth East Suffolk Regiment of Foot (12)
1/fourteenth West Yorkshire (Prince of Wales Own) Regiment of Foot
(14) 1/seventeenth Leicestershire Regiment of Foot (17)
1/eighteenth Royal Irish Regiment of Foot (18)
1/21st Royal North British Fusiliers (21) 1/22nd
Cheshire Regiment of Foot (22) 2/24th
Warwickshire Regiment of Foot (24)
1/25th Kings Own Borderers (25)
1/28th North Gloucestershire Regiment of Foot (28) 1/29th

Worcestershire Regiment of Foot (29)

1/33rd Yorkshire West Riding Regiment of Foot (33) 1/34th
Cumberland Regiment of Foot (34)

1/39th Dorsetshire Regiment of Foot (39)

2/40th Somersetshire (first visit) Regiment of Foot (40-1)

2/40th Somersetshire (second visit) Regiment of Foot (40-2)

1/41st Welsh Regiment of Foot (41)

1/43rd Monmouthshire Regiment of Foot (45)

1/46th South Devon Regiment of Foot (46) 1/47th
Lancastershire Regiment of Foot (47)

1/48th Northhamptonshire Regiment of Foot (48) 1/50th
West Kent (first visit) Regiment of Foot (50-1) 1/50th
West Kent (second visit) Regiment of Foot (50-2)

2/51st Yorkshire West Riding Light Infantry Regiment of Foot (51) 1/57
West Middlesex Regiment of Foot (57)

1/58th Rutlandshire Regiment of Foot (58)

1/61st South Gloucestershire Regiment of Foot (61) 1/62nd
Wiltshire Regiment of Foot (62)

1/63rd West Suffolk Regiment of Foot (63)

2/65th Yorkshire North Riding Regiment of Foot (65)

1/68th Durham Light Infantry (68)

1/70th Surry Regiment of Foot (68)

1/73rd Royal Highlanders (1/73)

1/73rd Royal Highlanders (separate obligation) (1/73-
2) 2/73rd Royal Highlanders (2/73)

73rd Invalids (INV)

1/74th Assaye Regiment of Foot (74)

1/77th East Middlesex Regiment of Foot (77)

1/80th Staffordshire Volunteers Regiment of Foot (80)

1/91st Argyleshire Highlanders (91)

1/96 Manchester Regiment of Foot (96) 1/99th
Lanarkshires Regiment of Foot (99) 1/102nd

Regiment of Foot (102)

102nd Invalids (INV)

Ceylon Rifle Regiment (CRD)

Military Pensioners Detachment (MPD)*

eleventh Mounted Police (11MP)

eleventh New South Wales Military Mounted Police (11NSWMP)*

28th Mounted Police (28MP)

51st Mounted Police (51MP) 80th

Mounted Police (80MP) 99th

Mounted Police (99MP)

Command Headquarters (HQ)

New South Wales Corps (NSWC)

Royal Artillery (not in any case under their joined unit) (RA) Royal

Engineers (RE)

twentieth Royal Sappers and Miners (Western Australia) (20RSM)

Royal Sappers and Miners (South Australia) (RSM)

Royal Hospital (RH) Royal

Staff Corps (RSC) Royal

Survey (RS)

Royal New South Wales Veterans Corps (RNV)

first Veterans Company Regiment of Foot (1VC)

second Veterans Company Regiment of Foot (2VC)

second Royal Veterans Battalion Regiment of Foot (2VB)

fourth Royal Veterans Battalion Regiment of Foot (4VB)

eighth Veterans Battalions Regiment of Foot (8VB)

<u>WARNING</u>

I can't give an affirmation that this rundown incorporates each warrior. This record was ready from the payrolls. There were independent month to month summons. Nonetheless, these summons are presently not surviving for all units nor for the entire time frame covered by this work.

The procedure used to extricate each warrior's name shifted from one record to another, unit to unit. This was a result of the varieties made by paymasters in their finance development. A few paymasters utilized various structures which featured all finance changes in a single specific spot. Most others however simply positioned a fighter on the finance toward the start of the payroll interval with practically no documentation that this trooper was a new contestant on that rundown. Where the officer was being paid before that is impossible to say. Paymasters seldom noticed the justification for finance changes which incorporated the justification for the section of a trooper for the first time.

Some soldiers were paid some place yet it was exceptionally normal found that there were holes between a warrior's finance record. There were neighborhood unit payrolls yet these ought to have been copied on the primary finance and unit assemble in many occasions. A portion of the nearby payrolls were checked against their mom unit's finance and a couple of officer's names were viewed as absent from one or the other record. Had both neighborhood and mother unit's payrolls been referred to reliably all through the examination stage, the work would have required one more year to finish (which I was not ready to give) and would have yielded something like three further names each year north of a long term period.

The truth of the matter is that because of the progression of time the finance readiness methods were lost, regardless of the rules being set out in the structures. Regardless every paymaster did it as he would prefer. None were steady. So the full picture on payrolls couldn't be perceived. Nonetheless, the picture mirrors that a few soldiers were taken care of finance elsewhere for a portion of the time they were in Australia. Appropriately, a portion of these individuals might not have being distinguished during the examination exertion. One fighter was gotten from a headstone. He was never found recorded on any payroll covering his unit's administration in Australia.

There are numerous sections in this work which were information entered as the names were seen to have been. It took amplifying classes, overwriting, utilization of highlighters, "whiteing-out" of reviewers' ticks, correlation with different sections, recreating the names from the passages in sequential request above and underneath it and defeating numerous different challenges to decipher names.

Many of the enduring records were in helpless condition when they were miniature shot. Blotching from the rotting of the paper hampered the perusing system as well. A few records were ineffectively shot. The foundation on the records of one regiment was practically dark. It was very difficult to endeavor to peruse the names recorded. It ordinarily took me hour to information - enter 130 soldiers. That regiment required 20 names each hour. There were likewise a few payrolls that were excessively light to read.

The focal point on some miniature film perusers couldn't be acclimated to peruse the picture unmistakably. A few apparatuses didn't consider perusing of the full page and on many events glare from encompassing lights was gravely filtered.

Many of the paymasters in the British Army composed with a lovely hand however some wrote in such little composing that it couldn't be perused even with an amplifying glass. Some composed over the separating line hence annihilating pieces of letters. Different recorders decorated their composing style with misrepresented twists and turns to where the letters couldn't be recognized. Many names couldn't be recognized concerning whether there was one letter or even three letters in each character. There were various inspectors' ticks which had converged with a portion of the names, adequately mutilating them.

"i"s were not generally spotted and "t"s were not generally crossed. Subsequently there might be more "e"s and "l"s than there ought to be. Many names were spelt uniquely in contrast to finance to finance, adding to the disarray. Some given names were changed on schedule. For instance one private was on the other hand called "William Francis Crofton" and "William Frederick

Crofton". I don't know how many times the payrolls showed someone named Daniel and later indicated David. Dominick, Daniel and Damien were often interchanged. "O"s and "Mc"s often went in and out of fashion. Burns/Byrnes, Rielly/Riley/Riely, Woods/Wood, Johnson/Johnston, Clark/Clarke, etc. were mind benders.

One paymaster, of the 40th Regiment, ventured to such an extreme as to put his own translation on the spelling of certain warriors' names. He was unable to spell just as his archetype. Disarray won. He absolutely affected some sensational changes in the records.

One trooper served in four units. He was purified through water Patrick Joyer and covered under that name. There is no such individual recorded in any payrolls. His chronic number in one of his regiments was record freely. This was checked. In each finance he was recorded as Patrick Joyce. He ultimately moved from the Military Police (British Army) to the NSW Police. His Police record says Joyer. What can one do?

Instances were located where the chronic number appended to an officer was not the equivalent on the following finance. So this strategy for checking personalities must be deserted not long later it was first used.

Almost all officers were first entered on the finance toward the start of their first payroll interval with their separate unit here. In any case 50% of the regiment would have shown up unpredictably and ought to have been paid in like manner. Maybe there was a bookkeeping chief included identifying with the terminal's finance. However, for the scientist that acts issues like to the genuine dates of beginning of administration in Australia. The framework proposes that the officer might have been paid in Australia for periods when he was indeed in England or somewhere else. One warrior was recorded as pensioned off at 1/6d outlay. The finance of one more regiment in another province demonstrated him to be on connection and as yet gathering his compensation from their paymaster, I may add while on debilitated leave and furthermore while running a plantation and prospecting for gold. I trust I don't need to discount any excessive charge. The trooper was my incredible extraordinary incredible grandfather.

Normally, there were separations, positioned independently from the principle body, with their own payrolls. Notwithstanding, the provincial base camp would for the most part remember these staff for its payroll.

The finance for the 39th Regiment incorporated the Officers and senior NCO's just a single time in seven years. The personality of certain officials was just found among their stipend payments.

The 77th Regiment's Officers and NCOs were totally unique between two connecting payrolls. It showed up briefly that the two records didn't identify with a similar regiment. Nonetheless, it was seen that the rundown of drummers and the privates were comparable. More is said about different characteristics including this unit further on. This was an extremely abnormal situation.

Where I experienced challenges interpreting composing I needed to make decisions. I might have recorded a few names wrongly. I continually referred to the Sydney Telephone Directory to check whether a few names I had observed really existed. A few names, which I had not before known about previously, were really affirmed in the phone registry. I bet everything I found in the index were relatives of the warriors I found. Now and again it took examinations with three separate payrolls to get the spelling correct.

Many family name spellings are off-base. I chose however from the beginning that where I tracked down the spelling "inaccurate", I would not transform it. Assuming I changed the spelling then I expected that an analyst could never observe the name which I planned to note back to the first record.

Not each finance was checked. I would begin my finance check with officials and afterward go through to privates at A, B and M. Assuming there were no progressions then I would skirt that record and continue to the following. This happened frequently. There might have been a few soldiers missed via this procedure. Had I done if not then this work would have required one more year to complete.

If anyone thinks that the person, the subject of their research was a British soldier in Australia and New Zealand, do not give up if at first you cannot find them. In that event may I suggest that you put the person's name on the top of a piece of paper. Then rewrite it below as many times as you can think of. Each time write it down differently. Alter a "K" to a "C" or a "C" to an "S". Substitute "U", "N", "M", "I", "E", "O" for each other. Double some letters such as "L" and "O". If Irish, add an "O" or "Mc" or delete them if the use later was the opposite. At least pronounce the name phonetically then write it down as it is pronounced. Eg., McFarland = McPharlan, Farrer = Pharoah, Dwyer = Dwire, Dunn = Done, Egan = Eagar.

If the researcher cannot find the correct given name. Do not give up. Also keep in mind that many people did not always use their baptismal or given name.

Please remember too that the troopers with families were joined by their spouses and youngsters. While most British warriors continued on, many returned as travelers. An extremely enormous number of troops took their releases in Australia. It is assessed that 3,000 soldiers kicked the bucket in Australia while on assistance and a further 9,000 soldiers just as 4,000 relatives stayed in Australia.

There were an expected 3,000 spouses and 6,000 kids in Australia with British Army families. The figure was tried on the first Royal Marines, the New South Wales Corps, fourteenth Regiment and eighteenth Regiment. Units went through as long as 12 years in Australia. So certain individuals who showed up as youths were grown-ups when their dad's unit was later re-posted. Many remained on in Australia or New Zealand and established their own families here.

Quite a couple of the passages just showcase the initials of the individual. The majority of the Officers were just recorded in the finance in that way. There were not very many non-charged staff who were recorded via initials. It may very well be added that a work was made to recognize the full given names of the officials and around half were found and adjusted
accordingly.

Rank was discarded as a large number of them changed their position occasionally. It was concluded that specialists would be best returning to the archives and checking all sections for the name of the individual they look for instead of zeroing in the finance on, say an Officer or a Corporal.

In many cases the finance uncovers that there were a few people with a similar name. Generally, the paymaster put a number later the passage, behind the given name. Try not to be tricked into imagining that Private Thomas Jones (4) on appearance of the unit in Australia was a similar Thomas Jones (4) when it left. On the off chance that one Thomas Jones was moved or released and another Thomas Jones was enrolled then another person became Thomas Jones No.4. The trooper who continued on might really have been No. 1 on the last past finance. In actuality there is no steady connection between an officer portrayed by an organized number put later his last name. Recall that the paymaster was just saying that he was paying four fighters named Pte. Thomas Jones. Later around 1840 the chronic number should assist with knowing each correspondingly named soldier.

There are numerous duplications. Where an officer was advanced or downgraded, he would unavoidably be shown twice or in uncommon occurrences, threefold. The last sequential records were checked for duplications. Where an individual had a similar uncommon name returning a few times in similar regiment, his entrance was decreased to one. Ordinarily named people were left untouched.

There is a risk here. Measurably one can't utilize the last figures with precision since certain soldiers were not indeed a similar individual recorded. There were a few cases recognized where the soldiers recorded with a specific name were in all actuality at least two unique people. There were three cases viz., in the NSW Corps, 102nd Regiment and the 73rd Regiment, where the men moved however a second individual with a similar name showed up sooner or later. They were James Walbourne, Gabrielle Huon and John Nowland. On checking they were all fathers and children and, as it turns out, every one of the children were Australian born.

There are around 500 soldiers recorded a few times since they were similar people serving in a few units.

Many fighters were paid on the finance of another unit and not on their own units' finance. It is conceivable that a few soldiers were missed on the grounds that they were paid on another unit's finance. It is expected that a few soldiers were never paid on their own unit's finance for the entire time they were positioned in Australia. This idea emerged on the grounds that on checking finance to finance it was seen that a few soldiers were missed off a few payrolls. However they were positioned in Australia. Others were overlooked from a few payrolls. An absence of coherence was taken note. They probably been paid some place. Except if obviously they returned to England since they were convict escorts.

Given my technique I earnestly accept that I have found the records for practically all the British units which served in Australia during the pilgrim period. I presume that there were some others as a result of cross references found and the notice in reports and abstract works of some different units and their staff. For instance, there was region leaders' report found (Ballarat) yet the official concerned was not referenced in any finance references. Official reports on the Eureka occurrence uncovered no less than four in any case unrecorded officials, including a Major General Nicholls.

It is hard to acknowledge that there were no mounted guns units in Australia before 1845. A significant number of the batteries and weapons are still set up. Engineers were most certainly here in light of the fact that they are cross referred to their payrolls however autonomous finance records found for Engineers before 1837 covered just five personnel.

One unit expert analyst really look at her records against mine. While she observed four contrasts, two were really record in there, the third was a spelling botch in the Army's finance and the fourth individual had been situated by the analyst from a graveyard tombstone, not from a payroll.

The arrangements of two units have been distributed. I contrasted my rundowns and them and observed no names missing from those different records. My records of two different regiments were freely looked at. My rundown of first armada marines was checked against a few different records. This list has 17 more marines then elsewhere recorded. The odd part about this is that the lists of sources are the same.

I truly accept that exclusions through administrative blunder or oversight ought not surpass 5% of the genuine records of any one unit.

As names fluctuated in spelling from one finance to another and given names were some of the time changed among payrolls, it would not be reasonable for me to acknowledge liability regarding exclusions or errors for confusion or oversights emerging from this predicament.

J. H. DONOHOE.
SYDNEY NSW

RESEARCH METHODOLOGY

Eight separate lists and references were utilized to find the regiments and some faculty. These were;

Index to War Office payrolls in Australia held in the Public Records Office.

War Office Records Index.

Index to War Office papers held in the Public Records Office.

Mitchell Library, State Library of New South Wales, List of Marines in the First Fleet

Ericson's Dictionary of Western Australia

McNicol's History of the Royal Engineers in Australia

Tippings Convicts Unbound

Stanley's Remote Garrison

Between them these records were not predictable. The rundown sheet at the front of the Index to War Office payrolls held in the Public Records Office was lacking and misdirecting. The War Office file demonstrated that 28 units served in pioneer Australia. There were really 90 British Army units, which served in Australia.

The War Office Records Indexes were extremely enlightening. A significant part of the material related to New Zealand notwithstanding the way that it said "Australia". There was no intentional endeavor to reject New Zealand. Truth be told where the information was blended, the New Zealand based soldiers were incorporated. As this activity was pointed toward observing Australian precursors, troops who just served in New Zealand were not especially sought after. As it turns out, a bigger number of troops served in New Zealand than in Australia later 1850 and some significant units just served there.

The Index to War Office papers held in the Public Records Office is a colossal reference yet it very well may be overwhelming.

Literary works, including reference book and the catalogs for different unit accounts and military examinations, were obtained for additional pieces of information about faculty in the British Army. These were generally useful. Reports and correspondence held in the Dixon Library were found and examined. The Minutes of the New South Wales Parliament and the Port Phillip Bay Council were referred to among them as were card records of the Tasmania State Archives. Major abstract works particularly those by Tipping, McNicol and Stanley were particularly useful.

Also referred to were the Victorian Lt. Lead representative's papers and Reports of the British Army into the Eureka riots.

The primary finance of every unit on their appearance was completely information entered. This was checked against the second and third ensuing payrolls and the increases were then included.

From then on the following three units were haphazardly checked for finance varieties identifying with staff starting on finance interestingly. Separation payrolls were once in a while verified that the work force recorded were really recorded on the central command's finance. One out of four payrolls was totally checked to guarantee that no work force were missed.

Where staff from different units were found these soldiers were inquired to their unique unit. Assuming that unit was not positioned in Australia, another record was initiated and that document was mixed into the last sort.

There was no validation as such as the procedures used were self-checking. The eleventh Regiment, which unexpectedly, had the biggest unforeseen, was autonomously checked by a student of history having some expertise in that regiment. She just recognized two oversights. These people were just situated by the antiquarian from recognitions composed on their headstones. The finance spelling was distinctive for one of them and the other seems to have been a convict who had once served in the regiment.

AUSTRALIANS IN THE BRITISH ARMY

Prior to 1820 Australians and British were enlisted into the privately based military units. It is assessed that 60 Australian conceived chaps enrolled locally and a further 120 convicts and travelers enrolled in Australia. These Australians may be found in the New South Wales Corps, 73rd Highland Regiment and 48th Northamptonshire Regiment. Some might have fill in for troops taking early release in Australia, particularly in the eleventh North Devonshire Regiment.

It ought to be referenced that the principal selection of an Australian happened in 1791 with the enrollment of Drummer Francis Spencer, matured 1 year 3 months. Before the experts argue and demand proof when they notice that his name is not listed in the payrolls until his seventh birthday, it should be pointed out that this reference was taken from two separate reports both of which were signed by the Corps' Adjutant at the time, then Major George Johnston.

After 1820 soldiers were for the most part selected in England and Ireland. It was impractical to distinguish Australian volunteers as no extraordinary notice is made of them in the payrolls. In any case, an officer could purchase right out of the military for an expense of twenty pounds. There is proof that a warrior could purchase right out of the military before his time was done at a lower expense. This happened when the trooper, looking for a release, enlisted a satisfactory substitution. The present circumstance can be identified, despite the fact that with impressive trouble, via the chronic number. The substitution enlist later 1820 will have the very chronic number as that of the individual for whom he subbed. This was perceived by tests applied to the payrolls of the eleventh North Devonshire Regiment and the 40th Somerset Regiment (second tour).

There is some notice in abstract works to Australians being selected for the Maori Wars. This declaration didn't appear in the British Army payrolls. 2,500 Australians served in real life in the Maori Wars yet their units were solely Australian, not British.

THE FIRST AUSTRALIAN WAR SERVICEMAN

There were a few Australians who joined the Britisharmed powers before the finish of the Napoleonic Wars. It has been undeniably challenging to confirm their conflict administration. Be that as it may, one Australia has been found to have battled at Waterloo. He was Andrew David White/Moore. Andrew was brought into the world in

Sydney in 1793, the child of Surgeon John White of the First Fleet and Rachel Turner, a convict who showed up on the "Woman Juliana" in the Second Fleet.

Rachel later wedded Thomas Moore, a previous crew member of the convict transport "Britannia". Thomas is popular for his gift of the assets that assembled the Moore religious College at Sydney University. Andrew later took on his progression father's surname.

Andrew cruised for England with first fleeter, Captain Henry Waterhouse, on HMS "Dependence" in 1800 to live with his dad. Andrew moved on from the Royal Military College at Sandhurst and was authorized in the Royal Engineers. It was in this Corps that he saw activity at Waterloo. (This material was explored and given by Jean Feughelman of the Society of Australian Genealogists).

EDITOR'S BRITISH ARMY LINKS

The Editor plunges from James Squire, a convict who showed up in Australia in 1788 on the "Charlotte" in the principal armada. James Squire had been right off the bat indicted in 1774 for gouging and had been condemned to transportation to the American settlements. In 1777 he was back home. He was in a real sense recorded in a few works, including Jean Feugelman's postulation "Mine Host James Squire of Kissing Point" as a "period lapsed fighter" and that he had served in the "Mainland Army". The records of the New South Wales Corps (viz., Francis Spencer's record) say that he was a mariner and relatives guarantee that he was a marine. One artistic source makes reference to that Captain Arthur Phillip utilized Squire as a gatekeeper on the event on which he skewered at Manly, Squire was a convict. For what reason did Phillip trust a convict when he had 150

marines? During the episode, Aaron Davies, the other convict watch, ran off. Assistant moved between the Aborigines and Lt.Henry Waterhouse, so Waterhouse could help Phillip to a boat. Assistant would not take shots at the Aborigines notwithstanding the compromising circumstance. Assistant, truth be told gotten to know the Aborigines later. Popular Aborigine, Bennelong, really passed on when he fell into a fermenting tank at Squire's distillery at Ryde. Assistant covered him in the yard of his home. This mirrors the picture of a trooper experienced with native individuals. Given the occasions, Squire seems to have been a mariner by calling however an officer by convict default and most likely he served on the Indian boondocks in North America. This would unquestionably clarify why Governor Phillip utilized him in inclination to his marines for that mission.

The records of that time are along these lines voluminous and unindexed, so, it is thusly remarkably difficult to test further on this data. It was very normal for convicts to move to the Army. Conditions in the Army were really more brutal. In those days a convict for instance didn't normally confront passing over the span of their day by day schedule. The draw to enroll was that they got a programmed pardon and on the finishing of their term, which could be abbreviated by paying a charge as much as twenty pounds relying upon the part of the term served to date, or on the other hand assuming they were invalided, they could return home.

For James Squire to have finished a full term in the British Army inside three years doesn't appear to be conceivable except if he was injured in the American War of Independence or he purchased out. It is conceivable that he was at that point a warrior when he submitted the offense and he was permitted to get back to his unit where he finished his term right away thereafter. The records utilized in this work propose however the later would not have occurred. Without a doubt, this later extremely fruitful finance manager purchased right out of the army.

The Editor's extraordinary incredible extraordinary grandma's sibling, Francis Spencer, of the NSW Corps, 102nd Regiment and 73rd Regiment, was the initial Australian conceived selection into the British Army. James Squire was Francis Spencer's dad (recognized in James Squire's Will)
The Editor is likewise dropped from Corporal Michael Horan and Private John Morgan of the 99th Lanarkshire Regiment. Michael Horan and John Morgan are recognized in the book "Mary, Mary Breen Where Are You?" an account of a British Army family in Ireland and Australia (Minerva Press, London, 1995).

Michael Horan was brought into the world in Eglih, close to Tralee, County Kerry, Ireland in 1806, the child of John Horan and Mary Walsh. In 1826 he had a contact with a Castleisland colleen named Mary Breen, the little girl of 1797 Irish revolutionary pioneer, Denis Breen and his sweetheart, Catherine Brosnan. Denis had set out on the "Minerva" for life transportation to New South Wales as far as concerns him in the Wicklow uprising in 1798 however was exculpated prior to cruising. Michael Horan and Mary Breen had a little girl, Mary. Michael Horan is recorded in Australia as an individual from the third Regiment (the Buffs) yet he isn't recorded on its finance. Michael and his sibling James are additionally recorded in Australia in the 40th Regiment (while the Buffs were in Australia). He later re-enrolled in the 99th Regiments. Michael and Mary junior, joined by his significant other, Eliza Morton showed up in Australia in 1843. It just so happens, Michael's sibling, James, hitched Mary Breen's sister, Catherine. Michael was stationed, firstly, in Berrima, New South Wales, then Newcastle, Parramatta and later in Spring Bay (Triabunna), Eastern Tasmania. Eliza Morton's sibling, Thomas was additionally in the 99th Regiment. Michael's previous sweetheart is accepted to have been the convict of a similar portrayal who showed up on the convict transport, "Surrey" (1V), in 1842 as a day to day existence transportation convict following a conviction for illegal conflagration. Michael was lent to the eleventh Regiment as his term approached its expiry, however separated in wellbeing while joined to that unit.

Michael was released from the British Army in Hobart in 1850 and chose an ex-fighter's award in Lambing Flats (presently Young, NSW) where he set up a cherry plantation and later found gold. Michael was among those diggers who battled against the British Army there during the counter Chinese uproars. He kicked the bucket in Young in 1874. Eliza Morton kicked the bucket in Tumut in 1894. Mary Breen was acquitted on first June 1850 and is accepted to have hitched a previous armed force official,   John

Marshall (Lieutenant, 48th Regiment). John Marshall later asserted that he once attempted to capture John MacArthur. While such a man existed and the occurrence really happened, the Lt. John Marshall who endeavored to capture John Macarthur was recorded as a Naval Officer. The records might be misdirecting. The 48th Regiment's finance uncovers that it had a Lt.John Marshall who was for all time positioned on convict ships. He was especially recorded for his empathetic treatment of convicts and it was over this issue that Lt.Marshall conflicted with MacArthur. It is held that he mediated in an episode wherein he observed MacArthur attacking a convict. A few parts of this story were found among records. So this John Marshall might have been a similar individual. The couple got comfortable Canowindra, New South Wales, where they had a child, John, who was more youthful than Mary's first excellent girl. Mary Breen passed on there in around 1884. Michael Horan's sibling, James served for the most part with the 99th Regiment in Western Australia.

Note! The connection between Michael Horan and Mary Breen has been energetically questioned by his relatives through his better half Eliza Morton. Michael's paternity of Mary Breen's little girl Mary is recorded in the contemporary registers of both the Castleisland Catholic Church and the Church of Ireland. Those records are surviving. Both John Morgan and Michael Horan were in a similar company in a similar remote spot while John was seeking his future spouse. Michael Horan then had custody of Mary Breen Horan. Approximately three ages later the Editor's family had reviewed this family ancestry which doesn't struggle with any enduring records. John Morgan and Mary Breen Horan's ensured Marriage Certificate explicitly specifies the 99th Regiment.

John Morgan was brought into the world in Temple, Cornwall, in 1826, the child of John and Phylis Morgan. He showed up in Australia as a support for the 99th Regiment in 1847. He served for a large portion of his term in Triabunna, Tasmania. He affirmed that he was an immediate relative of Sir Henry Morgan, the Elizabethan privateer. In 1851 John was indicted for renunciation (as in nonattendance without leave) and following his court military, which happened toward the finish of his initial term of military help, he was condemned to loss of his military benefits privilege. The story exceeds all expectations of administration terminated upon the arrival of his conviction. On hearing the decision he removed his uniform, given it over to the council individuals and left the British Army in his clothing. From the records that story appears to be conceivable. John got a tip of eighteen pounds on release and a proposal of a square of land in the state (this was a consolation to British warriors to stay on in the provinces as a non military personnel and furthermore as a reservist for protection purposes). The square offered was in Picton, New South Wales. Having no information about cultivating he immediately sold it. He then set up a small business in nearby Minto. Sadly, in 1862 John was confused with a relative of the lethal bushranger "Distraught Dog" Daniel Morgan, one of the state's most noticeably awful bandits ("Mad Dog" Morgan's genuine name was Staggs).

"Distraught Dog" changed his name in light of his profound respect for the pirate, Sir Henry Morgan, concerning whom he fantasized and endeavored to copy. The family needed to escape Minto. John purchased one more store at the side of South Dowling Street and Taylor Street, Darlinghurst, Sydney, inverse what is currently the Greek Community Center. The structure is still there.

John Morgan wedded Michael Horan and Mary Breen's girl, Mary, in St. Joseph's Catholic Church, Hobart, Tasmania in 1848. They had five kids. The oldest of John Morgan's kids was Louisa. Louisa's child, Edward James "Jim" Egan, was a power behind the production of the L.J. Prostitute Real Estate realm. Les Hooker and Jim Egan were accomplices in a joint endeavor when the firm "L.J.Hooker Pty Ltd" initiated and Jim Egan's business, which centered around a steady income lease roll, was genially consumed into it. Jim was additionally an impressive power behind the early improvement of Holy Cross College, Woollahra and Christian Brothers College, Waverley. A window at the back of the raised area (left side confronting) of Holy Cross Church recognizes Louisa Egan (nee Morgan) and on the plaque at the entry to Waverley College' Chapel recognizing promoters, the name "Mrs.J.Egan" is recorded (Jim Egan's better half). The proofreader was named James after this man. John Morgan's incredible grandson, Cyril Egan (1897-1961), was Dux of Waverley College in 1914. He was Captain of the College 1913 and 1914. Cyril imagined, planned and regulated the development of Sydney's Warragamba Dam. He is remembered in the book "Treat" (distribution forthcoming). Cyril Egan presented with the second Machine Gun Squadron in the first AIF's Lighthorse 1917-1919.

John Morgan passed on of cerebrum growth in Darlinghurst, in 1865, matured 39. His better half, Mary Breen Horan, passed on in Darlinghurst in 1881 of Hepatitis.

Other relatives oF JaMes Squire, Michael Horan and John Morgan incorporate Dr.Frank Egan who was among the main Australian clinical experts to spearhead the utilization of needle therapy close by current medication, Rev.Father Roderick Payne O.F.M., Asia and Pacific Provincial of the Franciscan Order of Friars, Collette Livermore, previous associate to Mother Therese of Calcutta and Michael Donohoe, one of the world's driving musicians.

Each regiment left behind in Australia around 250 men. During the exploration stage it was fascinating to see the uncommon family names of some extremely well known Australians. Did they dive from a pioneer time British officer too?

<u>SHIPPING</u>

Some of the payrolls uncover the name of the boat of appearance. This happens in with regards to a fourth of the appearances. There are additionally several regiments where the boat of flight is referenced too.

Countless soldiers showed up as escorts on the convict transports and the records now and again uncover the fighters' personality yet seldom the name of the vehicle. There would be a couple of cases where the date of appearance of the trooper and the vehicle can measure up. The Editor has independently distributed a work "The Bibliography of the Convict Transports" which shows the names of the convict transports and their date of appearance. It very well might be valuable to specialists for this purpose.

The Army staff referenced in this work were fundamentally obtained from the British Army payrolls of the time while the units were taken from a rundown outfitted by the Public Records Office in Kew, England. The Musters referenced a lot a greater number of troops than the payrolls recorded and the
transport landing records showed some more. A few Regiments as not among those recorded on the Public Records Office list. No clarification for this exclusion not really settled other than to recommend that these soldiers were traveling, on the way to or from, say India. Luckily, the Scribes recorded a considerable lot of the arrivals of these soldiers by name and they have been added to this work. Numerous different soldiers showed up as escorts and a considerable lot of their names and units were recorded. They also were added to this work.

Notation was made where Detachments showed up and were recorded exclusively by their Regiment. The Regiments concerned and their boat of appearance are;

fourteenth Regiment Lord

Wellington 1820 seventeenth
Regiment Tottenham 1819
24th Regiment Daphne 1819
24th Regiment Lord Wellington 1820
30th Regiment Atlas 1819
30th Regiment Lord Wellington 1820
34th Regiment Atlas 1819
34th Regiment Lord Wellington 1820
34th Regiment Tottenham 1819
45th Regiment Atlas 1819
46th Regiment Agamemnon 1820
46th Regiment Atlas 1819
46th Regiment Governor Macquarie 1817
46th Regiment Lord Wellington 1820
46th Regiment Tottenham 1819
47th Regiment Agamemnon 1820
48th Regiment Admiral Cockburn 1819
48th Regiment Guildford 1820
48th Regiment Surrey 1819
48th Regiment Tiger 1822
53rd Regiment Agamemnon 1820
53rd Regiment Atlas 1819
59th Regiment Agamemnon 1820
59th Regiment Daphne 1819 59th
Regiment Tottenham 1819 67th
Regiment Agamemnon 1820 67th
Regiment Tottenham 1819 69th
Regiment Agamemnon 1820
69th Regiment Lord Wellington 1820
69th Regiment Tottenham 1819
73rd Regiment Tottenham 1819
82nd Regiment Agamemnon 1820

83rd Regiment Agamemnon 1820

84th Regiment Shipley 1819

84th Regiment Surrey 1819

87th Regiment Daphne 1819

87th Regiment Tottenham 1819

89th Regiment Atlas 1819

89th Regiment Lord Wellington 1820

Bombay Marines Regiment Hunter 1817

Many of the soldiers from prior appearances can be perceived in this work where the boat of appearance, where referenced, was the name given by the warrior when recorded in an assemble or from an abstract source.

CONVICT ESCORTS

Convict transport accompanies in transit to the Australian states are not all around reported. The payrolls do uncover a portion of these soldiers. In any case, the

odd officer from a unit not presented on the Australian settlements is once in a while referenced in the finance of one more unit positioned in Australian provinces. From this it very well may be accepted that he had shown up as an escort and just gathered his compensation from the closest armed force unit.

Troops moving to the states were normally doled out convict escort obligation where their developments harmonized. Notwithstanding, moving soldiers and fortifications were not generally accessible as convict accompanies. It has been estimated that soldiers from any unit of the British Army were utilized as convict accompanies where moving soldiers couldn't be relegated. These soldiers were not coordinated with a provincial regiment and got back to Europe on the following accessible ship.

It has been recommended that they were not billeted with troops presented on the settlements. While anticipating return to Europe these soldiers bivouacked on Cockatoo Island in Sydney Harbor. The Editor couldn't confirm this point yet it very well may be correct. The individuals who gathered their compensation from the nearby regiment are recorded in this work.

The regiments of a few soldiers were viewed as referenced among the payrolls of different regiments here. Their regiments were not positioned in Australia. These regiments were the:1/fifth, 1/22nd, 1/24th, 1/25th' 1/29th, 1/33rd, 1/34th, 1/41st, 1/43rd, 1/45th, 1/61st, 1/62nd, 1/68th, 1/70th, and 1/73rd (separate Regiments), 1/74th, 1/91st, Royal Hospital Corps, second Veteran Company, Ceylon Rifle Regiment,

<u>ARTILLERY UNITS</u>

The enduring records on the British Artillery don't reflect the chronicled picture. The records found were joined, with impressive frustration, in this work with a solid detecting of exclusions. This was on the grounds that the work was expected to zero in on Australia, not explicitly New Zealand, yet that was the place where the units covered by the greater part of the enduring records were positioned. Ideally, in any case, New Zealanders may get some help from the consideration of these records in this work.

Lieutenant William Dawes, later whom Dawes Point on Sydney Harbor was named, is referenced in abstract sources as an artilleryman. He is in this work simply because I was aware of him from school days. His records as an artilleryman didn't appear. Regardless he was a Marine and McNicol says that Dawes' undertaking was engineering.

The work goes into distribution with the authentic goal of seeking after the Australian records further and, whenever found, remembering them for a later supplement.

<u>MOUNTED POLICE</u>

Contrary to certain misinterpretations about the starting points of the Mounted Police from whom a few Australian State's Police Services recognize the underlying foundations of their mounted troop, the Mounted Police were initiated by the British Army. The specific units and dates can't be straightforwardly recognized from the records since

Marines and the New South Wales Corps, just as line regiments, had mounted soldiers who were for the most part entrusted to complete police duties.

One of the principal units to fuse military mounted police was the 21st Royal Scots Fusiliers which doled out troops to mounted police work in New South Wales and in Western Australia between 1832-1839.

This was trailed by the 51st Regiment which gave mounted police in Western Australia somewhere in the range of 1838 and 1844.

The primary unit to consolidate a different expert unit of Mounted Police was the 80th Staffordshire Volunteers.

On the east coast and in Tasmania an organization of redcoats (around 100 faculty) and committed to mounted police work was framed from among the positions of the 1/99th Lanarkshire Regiment in 1842. The 99th Regiment moved out of the settlement in 1852 yet their Mounted Police Unit stayed behind and it became connected to the eleventh Devonshire
Regiment. The 1/eleventh Devonshires independently framed its own Mounted Police Unit, involved around 100 men, in 1852. Somewhere in the range of 1852 and 1854 there were indeed 2 units of Mounted Police, one framed of the leftover individuals from the 1/99th Regiment and the other of the 1/eleventh Regiment. They were both under the order of the 1/11 Devonshires. By steady loss the 1/99th work force had everything except vanished by 1854. The leftover work force moved to the positions of the 1/eleventh Devonshires. From 1854 to late 1856 the 1/eleventh Devonshires unit of Mounted Police was elite to the provinces. In 1856, by steady loss, the Military Mounted Police was being progressively gotten rid of. Six stayed on strength up until September, 1856 having being disengaged to provincial non military personnel units for a brief period up until the unit left Australia. A portion of the later Mounted Police were appended to the 1/twelfth Suffolk Regiment.

Incidentally, the eleventh/99th Military Mounted Police battled at Eureka close by the twelfth Suffolk Regiment.

It may bear some significance with note that the Royal Canadian

Mounted Police was begun in 1877. The Western Australian Mounted Policemen were granddads by then.

NATION BUILDERS

The British is more reviewed today for monitoring convicts. Presumably that is the thing that they did generally. Peace and lawfulness was their need and watching convicts was embraced by this function.

They likewise battled the bushrangers and did a damn steady employment of it. The bushranging wars that followed the dashes for unheard of wealth arose as the British Army, hindered with the Maori Wars, moved nearby lawfulness requirement to the neighborhood individuals. Local people couldn't do as great a task of it for quite a while. Truth be told it was British Army veterans staying in Australia who aligned the neighborhood police and made the framework work.

When all else fizzled in the Aborigine Border War in Queensland, the British Army ventured in.

One of the best accomplishments throughout the entire existence of pioneer Australia were the pilgrim public structure arranged in significant urban areas and towns. Victoria dormitory in Sydney is an exemplary illustration of splendid British Architect. The engineers, and developers for some situation, were past style British warriors. One of the pilgrim Australia's most splendid draftsmen was Lt.Colonel George Barney of the Royal Corps of Engineers. Barney later joined the New South Wales Civil Service where he headed the Lands Department. One of the main Commissioners of the New South police was previous Private henry Zouche of the fourth Regiment.

It was the British Army that planned and fabricated the New South Wales and Victoria Railways...Don't fault them for the distinctive rail measures. The government officials made that wreck and the British Army documents censuring the choices are very thick.

EARLY COLONIAL ARMIES

It is frequently said in recorded circles that before 1870 all provincial military units were involved only of volunteers. Not so!

From 1852 the pioneer state run administrations had an organization of paid soldiers for their own utilization. These soldiers were gathered from the positions of the British post powers and connected to a unique organization. The soldiers were exaggerated and they were extra to approved strength.

The separate pioneer states met the finance straightforwardly and the records of the 1/eleventh Devonshires and the 1/12 Suffolks recorded the exchanges which unmistakably distinguish the soldiers concerned.

ENGINEERING UNITS

Vague references to Engineers were found yet not many explicit unit payrolls were found. The records propose that the Artillery payrolls were incorporated with the Engineer's records.

Literary references demonstrate that the Engineers served between 1835-1870 and the Sappers and Miners between 1837-1870. A large portion of the work force couldn't be situated on the enduring payrolls. McNicol's work was referred to for this section.

This is unfortunate since it was the Royal Corps of Engineers that really fabricated pioneer Australia's business foundation, including the New South Wales railways.

More is merited being said in acknowledgment of their accomplishments in Australia.

DEATHS/KILLED IN ACTION

The British Army in the Australian Colonies was "on-administration". The British Army lost 9% of enrollments in World War 1. Incidentally the British Army's frontier powers in Australia lost a similar rate, ie., from all causes.

The British Army in Australia reliably lost 2 men for every brigade every month and numerous others were released as invalids, just to pass on in the blink of an eye a while later. Of the assessed 35,000 British soldiers who served in Australia, roughly 3,000 soldiers kicked the bucket here while on servic, from different causes. In an article in "Plummet" (Society of Australian Genealogists, September, 1995) on the destiny of the first British Marines in the Australian states, the writer referenced the stunning demise pace of 11.4% north of three years. These setbacks were considerably higher than those of the British Army in World War 1.

Numerous troopers were killed in pursues with convicts. Many troopers protecting convicts were killed, some withering of horrifying injuries. Scores were suffocated in get away from pursuits. Natives and bushrangers killed a few warriors who were protecting the local area from the odd attack. Indeed the primary trooper killed on assistance in Australia was Marine
Pte. Thomas Bullimore who was skewered by an Aborigine.

Four troopers were killed in real life during the Eureka insubordination. Notwithstanding the for the most part acknowledged view about the Battle of Eureka in Ballarat on twentieth December, 1854, in light of the one-sided work of Rafaello Carbonne, the action there by the British Army and the Police was in defence against an armed body of international adventurers and itinerants who were stealing funds due to the Victorian Treasury by evading gold mining licence fees (which Australian diggers were paying), nearly delivering the settlement bankrupt, just as taking the sheep and harvests of neighbors, requesting administrations for which they would not pay, for example, police, courts, streets and land concedes, and contributing essentially to the breakdown of peace and lawfulness in the locale. The supposed start of the resistance, ie.,the murder of Scobie at Bentley's Eureka Hotel, was actually a side effect of the pressure among local people and excavators, rather than an immediate reason for going rogue. Regardless it is clearly false that Bentley pulled off the homicide. He was really re-energized before the uprising later his inadmissible acquittal.

The inclusion among the rebel leaders of sincere law abiding people such as Peter Lalor distorts the image of the conflict. The seeds of an American takeover, like what happened in the Mexican areas of Texas and California a couple of years sooner, had as of now arose. Without a doubt a portion of the excavators were indeed similar people among those really liable for the ascent of American government in Mexican domain during the 1840s. Substantial evidence has been found that many of the miners were in fact veterans of the recently fought Mexican-American War which was a war where many modern American Historians acknowledge that the United States was the aggressor. Without a doubt the issues included are as yet touchy to the Mexican individuals who hold that piece of their nation was taken from them.

Peter Lalor was one of a minority gathering of dependable diggers who took the administration of the excavators from the troublemakers and agitators and inconspicuously downsized the hostility. Tragically, he didn't completely accomplish this on schedule to forestall the assault on the Stockade. So history has
tragically consolidated him with Eureka's mavericks or legends whichever inclination one takes.

The job of the British Army at Eureka was tied in with safeguarding neighborhood individuals and nearby issues, reestablishing the rule of law and reinstituting the progression of gold sovereignties so the genuine Government could pay for the administrations the dissidents were requesting for free.

Only one trooper, Private Mickey Rooney, was straightforwardly killed at Eureka. Mickey was shot through the head and kicked the bucket immediately. The other three fatalities were troopers who were injured however passed on of their injuries. Commander Wise of the 40th Regiment, for instance, was shot in the thigh and the arm. Barely deadly injuries! Indeed, he battled on. However, he passed on a couple of days after the fact. North of thirty diggers were killed.

Whilst the Eureka excavator's standard represents hatred of expert in debates and indicates to energize Australians to irate causes, actually no Australian battled for or with the diggers. Australians had greater partiality with the British Army which was safeguarding the privileges of the nearby Australian people group at the time.

The records demonstrate the accompanying sythesis of the Military, Naval and Police Force at Eureka:

Captain J.W.Thomas, Military Commander, Ballarat District.

eleventh/99th Military Mounted Police 30 staff Lt.Hall Lt. Gardyner

Port Phillip Mounted Police 70 staff Sub-Inspectors Fennell, Chomley and Cossack

Port Phillip Police Force 24 personnel

1/twelfth Suffolk Regiment 65 faculty Capt. Queade, Lt. Paul.

1/40th(2nd visit) Sommershire Regiment 87 staff Capt. Savvy, Lt. Bowdler, Lt. Richard

HMS "Fantome" Numbers not recorded

HMS "Electra" Numbers not recorded

Vandeimonien Police Numbers not recorded

The complete power was 276 staff, 100 mounted and 176 foot in addition to Royal Navy in gunnery support.

An early exertion was made in this work to record those British officers who kicked the bucket from whatever reason for death. The assignment turned out to be too troublesome and dialed back the accomplishment of the major objective.

Death declarations were given from 1856 and a portion of those located uncover that tuberculoses was the killer.

TRIVIA

British officers were by and large called "Red Coats". Nonetheless, that was not their nearby epithet. At home and in the provinces they were classified "Lobsters". One story exceeds everyone's expectations was propositioned by a fighter, an angry lady answered "I don't bubble lobster in my kettle,"

* * *

The Catholic Church in Australia was initiated by the British Marines. Originator of the Australian Catholic Church was Marine Sergeant William Baker. Sgt.Baker showed up in Australia with the First Fleet. He was the Orderly Sergeant to the principal Governor of New South

Wales, Captain Arthur Phillip. Sgt. Dough puncher got back to England with Captain Phillip yet he later relocated to Australia. He turned into the dad in law of Irish Rebel Leader, Michael Hayes, the spouse of William's little girl, Elizabeth Huffnell. Michael Hayes guided the Catholic lay in New South Wales without a trace of approved pastorate before the appearance of Rev. Father Peter Connolly (Fr.John Therry was not the primary approved Catholic Priest to show up in Australi. Indeed there was a Bishop, three Convict Priests and an unlawful outsider Priest before Fr.Therry showed up. Fr.Connolly was the senior of the initial two approved Priests.).

* * *

The British Army had troops positioned in Vandiemensland (Tasmania) in 1803 preceding the Marines showed up in 1804. The NSW Corps positioned a unit close to Devonport.

* * *

The British Army had troops positioned in North Australia as ahead of schedule as 1824. A company of the third Regiment of the Buffs was positioned on Melville Island.

There were additionally various stations dispersed all through North Australia that in any case would have been neglected. A portion of these strongholds, for example, Cape York, Fort Essington and Fort Dundas were monitored by Marines.

* * *

Governor William Bligh was truly captured by Corporal Michael Marlborough on the New South Wales. Michael, it presently appears, erroneously detailed that he needed to pull Bligh from under a bed. This established the monstrous fantasy that has since won. A free observer, Robert Campbell, gave an alternate form of the capture. Campbell said that Marlborough captured Bligh at the cafe table. Bligh and Campbell were both situated together at that point. John Palmer and Georg Suttor were likewise captured. Robert Campbell is reviewed as a careful and fair man.

* * *

The Catholic Church is Australia was prohibited until late 1819. One of the makes driving the British Government respecting tensions to permit Catholic ministry into the provinces was the endeavors of the men of the 48th Regiment which was qualified for a Chaplain however just 25% of its strength
was Protestant. So the Regiment looked for a Catholic Chaplain all things considered. The British Government compromised by approving neighborhood Priests accessible to the local area in general.

* * *

The British Army and their families contributed as much as 20% of the number of inhabitants in the Australian settlements up to 1830.

* * *

Possibly upwards of 20 Australians served in the Napoleonic War. Commander Coy's Company of NSW Corps which had a few Australians has been asserted by one scientist to have been appended to the eleventh Devonshires in Europe (Captain Coy's finance records have not made due). Six Australians served in Ceylon in 1813 with the 73rd Regiment and two served in Ambon in 1815 in the 100th Regiment earlier the 102nd Regiment). Lead representative Phillip Gidley King's Australian conceived child, Ensign Norfolk King, kicked the bucket on help at sea.

Among Australia's original conceived or child of a traveler or convict pre-1800, were at least;

Major-General 1
Rear Admiral of the Blue 1
Major 1
Captain 2
Naval Lieutenant.............2 (one from a convict family)
Naval Ensign*................3 (one from a convict family)

Privates.....................21 (practically all from convicts)
Sailors.......................2+

*Royal Navy Ensign Sydney King, child of first armada convict, Anne Hinnett, was presumably the principal Australia to pass on assistance when his ship
was soaked in 1837.

* * *

Huon pine doesn't honor Pte. Gabriel Lewis (Louis Huon de Kirrilieu) of the 73rd Regiment.

* * *

Two Privates in the British Army humiliated the Governor of New South Wales in 1826. The treatment of British soldiers in the early colonial days was so bad, indeed worse than that of convicts, that many of them committed minor offences so that they could be gaoled, then assigned and given the benefits than many ticket of leave men and emancipists enjoyed such as land grants, access to marrying or the ability to operate a business.

By the mid-1820's the plague of feelings among officers sabotaged the strength of the British Army. The Governor, Ralph Darling, chosen to make an illustration of the following fighter. Privates Joseph Sudds and Patrick Thompson of the 1/57th Regiment together took some fabric from a shop with the communicated expectation of being gotten, indicted and condemned to transportation. They accomplished their objective. The two men were condemned to seven years transportation, the base sentence. Rather than being doled out however, Governor Darling arranged that they carry out their punishment on a street posse and that they ought to be shackled by the legs and the neck. Sudds was a wiped out man and kicked the bucket in practically no time. There was a public objection and the British Government concluded that Darling had surpassed his abilities by modifying the sentence of the court. Thompson, as it turns out, was pardoned.

One shamefulness uncovered in the contemporary Army records about this occurrence, which has not in any case been generally referenced, was that the rort for which the two privates were rebuffed, one losing his life, begun among the sergeants who ought to have set a superior model. Clearly Governor Darling preferred putting the fault where the

buck halted rather than on the sergeants. Clearly Darling realized that sergeants are the military's best troopers so he singled out dispensables.

* * *

In 1861 the British Army in Australia almost did battle with itself. The province of Victoria was basically a free state (just 1,500 convicts were moved there). By 1861 18% of the number of inhabitants in Victoria was American and 70% was traveler, particularly Greek, German and Italian. At the flare-up of the United States Civil War, agreement reviews were taken in bars all through Victoria with respect to which side Victorians would take in the contention. The choice was predominantly for the Confederacy.

The British free migrants overwhelmed Victoria's neighborhood populace and were seriously faithful to Great Britain. Warmth among Britain and the new Confederacy, framed in terms of professional career joins, offered Britain another companion in North America. Then again the Union Army, with a majestic dream matching Britain's, represented a tactical danger to the Canadian states. This feeling blended in with the profound hatred among Americans, Greeks and Italians in Victoria towards the interruption into the Eureka question of 1854 by the British Government and the British Army into what was seen locally as basically neighborhood issues. These impacts, contrary energies as they were, caused those touched by the Eureka incident to empathise with the rights of the Southern States to resolve their local issues locally and thus they merged with Victoria's deeply loyal British community to sympathise with the Confederacy. Likewise the Americans realized that the annulment of bondage was just a short time. Regardless they didn't consider subjugation to be a significant issue in the withdrawal development of the occasions. They realized that financial aspects was the train of that common war.

Because of the delay for data to course through, the nearby American people group was not exposed to the Union publicity on the safeguarding of the association and the objective of a definitive loss of the slave

masters, which, regardless, didn't develop as a goal philosophy
until later the Battle of Gettysburg. So they set little significance on the slave issue. Without a doubt, five certified slave States favored the Union reason on the episode of threats. Another, Virginia, isolated its loyalties.

As referenced, the conflict was seen to relate more to economics and particularly the lucrative trade between some Southern States and Europe which was undermining trade opportunities in the South for Northern manufactured products and the cheaper procurement of Southern raw materials for Northern industry. The benefits of economy of scale utilising Southern raw materials favoured European manufacturers to the disadvantage of Northern manufacturers and this was seriously impacting on the delivery price of Northern goods in both all North American markets and in Europe. The Northerners needed the Southerners to lose their slaves, not really for moral reasons, but rather to constrain up work expenses and power up the European maker's cost of produced products in North America and hence drive them out of North American business sectors. The vehicle edges would ultimately lean toward the Northerners and give them the advertising edge. Victoria's nearby American people group, regardless of whether of Northern or Southern beginning, knew this. The disposal of subjection hypothetically would widen the prize driven work power among ex-slaves and consequently invigorated an extraordinary nearby purchaser society, which smiply put, implies greater neighborhood markets.

Significant to the issue was the job of the Greek people group in Victoria. The Greeks monitored a considerable lot of the exchanging ships on the Europe - USA courses, especially toward the South. Many had encountered the enslavement of their families by the Turkish Ottomans and they saw past the subjection struggle. They upheld the neighborhood American community.

In New South Wales there was an entirely different picture. Americans, for instance, were uncommon. Regardless most families living in New South Wales had been impacted by the convict transportation conspire. The residents knew straightforwardly of individuals mistreated by the framework which was seen by most neighborhood individuals as a type of subjection. The issue of bondage was of high repute to the hearts of all in this province and the nullification of servitude was paramount.
Besides, the neighborhood individuals were absolutely oblivious to

American financial aspects and indifferent with regards to it. The shamelessness of servitude overwhelmed neighborhood thought.

The British Army had, as per normal procedure, raised nearby volunteer army type units among exservicemen and among the militarily disposed residents. In any case, during the Civil War Sydney siders were so energetic with regards to their help for the Union reason thus distrustful with regards to a Confederate intrusion that long-lasting armed force billets and volunteer army postings were full.

This paranoia went so far as Sydneysiders even raising their own army for the defence of Sydney against the feared Confederates. The soldiers even wore Union Army style outfits. The unit strutted on Sundays and the motorcade comprised of a get together external a northern Sydney lodging, presently know as "Athol Hall" close to Taronga Park. Later roll call the men were excused and afterward completely suspended to soak up in the inn's cool refreshments.

One could feel that this situation would not frighten the Confederates whose standing for courage fighting far surpassed that of the Unionists who appeared to typically out-number the Confederates but, right off the bat in the conflict, lose so many of the fights and engagements. However the presence of this small clumsy power along with the feelings of the settlers was known in Confederate circles. It was additionally known to the Union Navy. It did in undeniable reality get the Confederates far from Sydney.

During the Civil War, the Union Navy barred Southern ports. The Confederates countered this by buying two enormous boats from their British proprietors. These boats were changed over into "Pillagers" which irritated Union mechantmen in worldwide waters. The boats were named the "Alabama" and the "Florida". The USS "Kearsage" cornerd the "Alabama" off the French Coast, and not a long way from the Isle of Wight, and sank it. English Yachtsmen protected the survivors and, beating the "Kearsage", they dashed them to wellbeing in Great Britain.

The Confederates purchased one more boat to supplant the "Alabama" and
referred to it the CSS as "Shenandoah". The "Alabama's" survivors

monitored the boat. In 1865 the vessel cruised into the Pacific where it zeroed in on the obliteration of the Union's whaling armada in the north Pacific. Albeit a cruising transport, the "Shenendoah" was likewise steam driven and was dependant upon the power blend for its quick in and out job. In March, 1865, towards war's end, the "Shenendoah" broke its motor drive shaft. The closest unbiased ports where docking and fix offices were accessible were Sydney and Melbourne. Albeit frantic, the "Shenendoah" had to cruise on past Sydney, since Sydney had a hostile multitude of fan hanging tight for it there. It continued to go all things being equal, the entire way to agreeable Melbourne.

Despite global law which permitted a fighting country's boats into an impartial harbor for just 24 hours, the "Shenendoah" remained for a considerable length of time. During that time its group was feted. It likewise enrolled one Englishman and 41 Australians, again a demonstration in opposition to worldwide law (just Charles Kenyon, the child of a British officer, gotten back to Australia). During this time however the British Army figured out how to get the arrival of all of the "Shenendoah's" Union detainees of war, which it accomplished by compromising neutrality.

The "Shenendoah" got back to the ocean and sank forty additional boats, and, for the most part later the Confederate chief, General Robert E.Lee, had surrendered.

In August, 1865, four months later Lee's acquiescence, the British Royal Navy halted the "Shenendoah" off the shoreline of China where papers must be created to persuade the Captain, James Wardell, and his group to stop threats. The "Shenendoah" then sailed for England and after entering Liverpool Harbour, its Captain surrendered it to the British Government.

A furious Union Government sued the Victorian Government for the unlawful accommodation gave to the "Shenendoah". This suite was important for the "Alabama" claims made against Great Britain for its help, as a nonpartisan nation, given to the Confederacy during threats which

harmed the Union conflict exertion. The cases were heard in the International Court of Settlement. In 1872 the matter was finalised and the Australian colony of Victoria was held responsible for the payment of four hundred thousand pounds in damages in favour of the United States Government.

On the finish of the "Alabama" claims and the rebuilding of cordial relations with Great Britain, the United States Government recalled the cloth labeled multitude of Sydney siders who had pursued off the "Shenandoeh". It chose to say "Thank you Sydney" and celebrate the endeavors to obstruct the Confederacy. The United States Government did this by despatching the USS "Kearsage" to Sydney. This was for sure a recognition for those challenging champions who truly impeded the "Shennedoah" arriving at Sydney.

In request to come to its meaningful conclusion the United States Navy even compartment the "Kearsage" just outside "Athol Hall" while it was in Sydney. While its common conflict group had headed off in various ways following the suspension of threats, the United States Navy had travelers on board the "Kearsage"..some of its unique team which sank the "Alabama", including its unique Captain. This was hence no normal altruism visit.

* * *

The Australian Colonial Armies initiated in 1870. The establishment unit was the first Battalion The eighteenth Royal Irish Regiment. In mid 1870 the along these linesldiers of this unit were offered the choice of a release or re-enrollment. A considerable lot of the people who took their release got comfortable Australia or New Zealand. The individuals who re-enrolled were given the choice of getting back or staying in Australia or New Zealand to serve in the frontier armed forces. A large number of the men stayed to serve locally, if necessary. In this manner finished the 82 years of the British Military presence in Australia and the chance to begin the Australian armed forces. Deplorably, the pilgrim Governments couldn't bear the cost of a guard spending plan, so, for the initial six years later the takeoff of the British Army from Australia's shores, the frontier units were stringently voluntary.

* * *

The impression is that the Along these linesldiers who served in a large number of the units which served in Australia were overwhelmingly Irish conceived. So, begorrah, on occasion Australia was attacked by an Irish Army. Top a' tha mornin' ter yur tar, sar. It been a great dei an oal. Ta be certain ta be sure.

* * *

Victoria Barracks in Sydney is the unrivaled delight of the Australian Army. It is a wonder in plan and still very stylish today. Its development started during the 1840s' and a significant part of the work was contracted. Cash was tight because of an extreme world financial downturn however development proceeded. To conquer cash deficiencies, the military squeezed troops of the twelfth Suffolk Regiment into working. They might have had other help.

In 1838 French Canadians defied their British rulers. The British Army crushed the renegades, balanced a significant number of the detainees and afterward despatched the survivors to Norfolk Island. The French Canadian dissidents showed up in Sydney on board HMS "Bison" enroute for Norfolk Island where the endurance pace of a convict or detainee was extremely low. For the individuals who persevered through the framework their life was abominable.

All however one of the 99 French Canadian Prisoners of War were Catholics. The defiance had its foundations in strict struggle between the pRevailing Catholic French Canadian people group and the restricted assigned powers from the British Government including neighborhood monetary undertakings. The Catholic Archbishop of Sydney, Rev.Bede Polding, was shocked at what lay ahead for them. He mentioned that the Prisoners of War be arrived in Sydney all things considered. At the point when the Governor denied, Polding requested that all victualling of HMS "Bison" stop. No water to be provided, no food, no fixes and no maritime stores to be stacked. The transcendently Catholic waterside laborers were told to guarantee that this declaration was followed and

that HMS "Bison' stay fastened to the wharf until it decayed where it lay. However, instead of confronting a neighborhood standoff, the Governor at last consented to land the French Canadians in Sydney.

They were passed on to their own assets. There was no cash for taking care of them nor detaining them. In this way, the French Canadians detained themselves in a shoddy gaol called the Longbottom Stockade at Habberfield. They gathered sticks and offered the kindling to bring in cash for their food. They gathered shells and squashed them to make lime for concrete. Sydney individuals upheld them by purchasing their produce.

In 1844 Queen Victoria excuse them and everything except one returned home. One had fallen head over heels for a Sydney young lady and remained behind to establish the Marceau line of Dapto.

There is a landmark to the French Canadians in Victoria Barracks and the legend wins that they assisted with its development. This reality is questioned by the Barrack's Historian. Never-the-less the fantasy makes due and it is referenced in the event the landmark was raised to recognize any commitment that the French Canadian Prisoners of war might have made to the structure of the Barracks.

***

As this work goes to press there is some uproar raised by Historians about the disclosure in Northern Australia in the mid 1830s by a tactical gathering drove by Lt. Richard Nixon, likely of the Madras Regiment, of a province of Dutch-Aborignal Australians whose family line included relatives of Europeans who had shown up before the British in 1788. A campaign was scanning regions around the Fitzroy River and Darwin for evidence.

In 1696 Mario Sega, an Italian sailor with the De Vleming endeavor escaped close to Rottnest Island off the coast from Fremantle. He came to Fremantle and lived with the neighborhood Aborigines. In 1756 a Dutch ship

sank off Rottnest Island and a Dutch young lady named Wilhelmina made due. Wilhelmina was protected by the neighborhood Aborigines and settled with the clan which included by then, at that point, relatives of Maria Sega.

Captain John Stirling arrived in Fremantle in June 1829 with a gathering of pilgrims. A tactical separation of the 21st Royal Scots (North British) Fusiliers was presented on Fremantle in help. This was a mounted police organization, driven by Lt.Nicholas Wrixon. Lt.Wrixon found a clan of Aborigines which remembered relatives of Mario and Wilhelmina for what is currently past midtown Perth. The Aborigines didn't vanish yet coordinated with the neighborhood pilgrims. There stays various Australians of their lineage. Lt."nixon's" association with Northern Australia emerged from some portion of the mounted police organization being presented on Melville Island soon after the finding of the Italian-Dutch Aborigines.

***

In 1857 the British unloaded right around a whole regiment in Australia. At that point there were a few regiments, including the eleventh, twelfth and 65th which had left upwards of 200 soldiers behind later the units' takeoffs. These staff had been kept on strength by each individual substitution unit.

In 1857 the British Army moved the 77th East Middelsex Regiment to Australia. The records uncover an additional a standard significant degree of abandonments not long after appearance in Australia. Not long after its appearance in Australia the unit released 127 staff. Inside 90 days of appearance in Australia some remaining soldiers from the left unit had been moved into the 77th Regiment. Along with the leftover soldiers from the withdrew units, the complete strength of the 77th Regiment since appearance arrived at very nearly 1,000 men. On tenth November, 1857 the regiment released practically every one of them including the vast majority of its the officials, Commanding Officer and Adjutant included. The most noteworthy enduring position was one single Captain. By January, 1858 the strength of the regiment was down to around 150 work force. Six officials (of 20) and eight sergeants

(of 25) just made due. The regiment was then moved to India where it was remade. As it turns out, the recuperated defectors were among the individuals who were not discharged.

The Public Records Office Indexes allude to papers surviving concerning the excusal of a Regimental Commanding Officer in Australia. These papers might identify with the 77th Regiment.

The eighteenth Royal Irish Regiment likewise directed a mass release practice in 1869. The situation here was quite different though. The Royal Irish Regiment was a significant piece of the withdrawal of the British Army from Australia. The records uncover that the men were given the choice of being released or moved elsewhere.

That circumstance seems to have come about because of an economy drive. This emerges on the grounds that it would have been more commonsense and financial for the British Army to have released those wishing to remain in Australia instead of driving them to return home at extraordinary cost.

This likewise supports the picture that the positioning of troops in Australia who were only brought into the world in the British Isles was one more method for decreasing Britain's expanding populace. Somewhere in the range of 1820 and 1870 Australians were just enrolled alternative for troops taking an early release, which was uncommon. With one of every three British fighters staying in Australia on release or move of their regiment, the plan worked.

SOLDIER'S ORIGINS

This work is presumably the principal complete investigation of the British Army in Australia. Conventionally, the specialists who have procured their abilities regarding this matter via inspecting will exhort that There is a simple method of observing the starting points of a warrior by following him through the payrolls until his release is found. There, they recommend, will be tracked down notice of his

spot of birth and his occupation at the hour of his selection. That is a word of wisdom. Nonetheless, don't be misled. The copyists just did that every so often. Passing and abandonment records overlook these subtleties. This information was likewise excluded when a warrior was needed to deplete his accumulated leave preceding release. These circumstances were all the more regularly the case. The data was here and there gave on an advancement or on renunciation too.

By the way, the reference to birth and occupation was generally made in the comments segment. Some regimental assistants, however, made the section around the trooper's name.

There are a couple of hints in the payrolls past the conspicuous which will assist an analyst with finding the beginnings of officer. Once situated for the time on finance, one can look out the finance for the unit's terminal in England for the past finance passage. The stop finance could affirm when the fighter was first joined up. Then check where the recruiting personnel were stationed at the time the soldier first appeared on payroll. There was normally something like six enlisting stations. Enlisted people would ordinarily have lived close to one of them.

Also of help is the chronic number. Really look at the officers with adjacent numbers. There are many examples of troops who had a similar family name. Father and children perhaps or even siblings and cousins. There are many episodes recorded where a few group with uncommon names just show up on payrolls of just one regiment and afterward there are a few of them and their chronic numbers border. The blend of given names could help recognize from records of the International Genealogical Index on account of a few comparable kin names with the equivalent parents.

Troops were enrolled from age 9 years old (Separate finance area for young men) and they were paid "men's wages from fifteenth birthday celebration. They could be completely pensioned at age 29 years (at 10/6d per week).

One intriguing point that arose during the exploration stage was the gathering of troopers of a similar uncommon name. This happen many times. This focuses to troop enrolling with companions, siblings and cousins. Assuming one can't find their own progenitor's subtleties, search for the subtleties of one more officer in a similar regiment with a similar last name, particularly one who had a nearby sequential number.

It showed up too that many substitutes had a similar family name. These individuals might have been father and son.

Also found were that the spouses of certain soldiers had similar last name by births as different troopers in the regiment. There was a normal of 500 relatives with each regiment. The supervisor plummets from a the trooper girl of a partner in his unit. There probably been a significant extensively number of relationships with the unit families.

Another wellspring of family connecting was the segment in the finance "Officers settlement of pay". Troopers could utilize the British Army finance framework to move cash anyplace on the planet. A trooper utilizing this office would recognize himself, uncover the name of the individual to whom he was moving the cash, the aggregate in question and the location of the planned beneficiary. The names of mums and fathers and young lady companions prevailed in this section.

CHELSEA PENSIONERS

There were considerable quantities of British servicemen released in Australia and countless them, who were released in different areas of the planet, moved to Australia.

Many of them were Chelsea Pensioners.

The records of these individuals have made due and will be the subject of another book. The records (unindexed) are held in the Mitchell Library, State Library of New South Wales.

THE PETTICOAT REBELLION?

According to an archive found among the payrolls of the New South Wales Corps, Corporal Michael Marlborough once announced recorded as a hard copy that he captured New South Wales Governor William Bligh. He said that when he captured Bligh he needed to haul him free from his bed. This report has been for the most part acknowledged by numerous understudies of the "Rum Rebellion" as right. One supporter portrayed the scene and that image remained on the site of the old Government House at the intersection of Bridge and Phillip Streets, Sydney for some years.

There is one imperfection however, Corporal Marlborough didn't specify that there were two individuals captured simultaneously. Presently how did two major men fit under Bligh's bed?

The other individual was Robert Campbell. Campbell was a

neighborhood money manager. His review was that Corporal Marlborough and a few different soldiers jumped into the lounge area of Government House and captured he and Governor Bligh at the feasting table. Campbell's story was acknowledged by the British Government who repaid him with a 4,00 section of land award close to Longford, Van Diemensland (Tasmania). Campbell moved the land to the editorial manager's extraordinary incredible extraordinary granddad, William Lucas, quickly afterwards.

Robert Campbell was a man of the greatest degree of respectability. While numerous understudies of the "Rum Rebellion" have projected defamations on Bligh, even Corporal Marlborough kept down with regards to Campbell's direct. In the event that Marlborough had remembered Campbell for his report, there couldn't have ever been any individual who might have trusted him, even concerning where his report related to Bligh. The oversight of any notice of Robert Campbell from Corporal Marlborough's report hence thoroughly ruins it.

Campbell's Canberra property "Duntroon" passed to the Australian Army where it presently houses the Royal Australian Military College and the Australian Defense Academy. If Robert Campbell foresaw the transition that emerged there in the twentieth century, then he would be a very proud man. The Australian Army is a lot tidier association for that
organization than the New South Wales Corps was without it.

Part of Governor Bligh's concern might have been on the grounds that the New South Wales Corps was being controlled by His Majesty, the King, actually. There are similarities of proof arising that King George 111 and his children, Prince Alfred, the Duke of Cumberland especially (not the butcher of Culloden), Prince William, Prince George and Prince Albert (Queen Victoria's dad) were straightforwardly involved in the exercises of the New South Wales Corps. There are various history specialists presently exploring this field and finding dubious data.

For instance, among the early reports connected to the Corps' records was a "half sheet". A "half sheet" was a term in the British Civil and Disciplinary Services for the calling of a report following an objection of a tactlessness or rule breech. The top portion of the sheet contained the topic of the speculated abnormality. The recipient was needed to clarify the circumstance on the base portion of the sheet. The topic demonstrated that the Officer answerable for getting sorted out the New South Wales Corps had acted conflictingly with orders made straight by the Army Chief of Staff. With all due respect the recipient said that he had followed up on different orders surrendered by somebody senior. Ruler Alfred was the Chief of British Armed Forces.

Possibly upwards of seven first fleeters were connected to the King. Transient, "James Smith", convicts, Olivia Gascoigne, Matthew Everingham and Nathaniel Lucas and crew members, Christopher Palmer, Henry Waterhouse and John Palmer can be connected genealogically to the imperial family. Afterward, a transient named "Thomas Jones" showed up. James Smith was obviously a bogus name and South African records demonstrate that this man was confused with King George 111 as a result of his similarity to the King. His quality in Western South Africa before his flight for Australia on the "Woman Penrhyn" was honored by the name of the town where he remained, "George Rex" which is presently called "George". Research is being embraced to set up whether this man was truth be told King George himself. This is questioned however never the less King George 111 entered a London center only preceding the flight of the principal armada in
1787 and re-emerged shortly after Mr.Smith's return to England. Mr. Smith was of the same age and appearance.

"Thomas Jones" has been shown to be a bogus name. Another pseudonym and his genuine name have now been found. "Jones" was recognized by contraSting a Coroner's Report into his dubious passing with the Parish register. No such individual was covered with regards to that time. St.Phillip's records uncover that the main individual covered that day and as long as after three days, was Joseph Waterhouse of whom there could be no other record in the state. This man was followed to the Waterhouse group of Yorkshire which a few ages prior were connected by union with the Royal family.

Descendants of first fleeter, Olivia Gascoigne, accept that she was identified with the Wentworth's, Earls of Strafford, whose previous age was hitched unto the Gascoigne family which unexpectedly had a part named Olivia before this.

Convict John Eddington was connected to the Earl of Haddington.

Matthew Everingham was connected through a marriage a few ages prior to the Wentworth's, Earl's of Strafford.

Evidence of cases that convicts were associated with the gentry were discredited at the time by first armada specialist Dr.White. Scholastics hold to Dr.White's recorded remarks. Dr.White was a specialist and a gynecologist yet he wasn't a genealogist. Regardless he was wrong!

Records of the Tooth (Brewery) family records uncover that this fermenting goliath's originator was the grandson of King George IV and Fanny Lucas of Thames Ditton. Fanny Lucas is referenced as the stupendous little girl of Princess Caroline. Fanny Lucas is accepted to have been the sister of first armada convict Nathaniel Lucas. Ruler George's records don't uphold this record however a Royal Historian remarked that King George IV was known for his excursions and the copyists could well have missed a few ill-conceived youngsters who were recorded by their families.

Crewman Henry Waterhouse's back up parent and maritime support was Prince Alfred, the King' sibling and the Army Chief of Staff. "Thomas Jones" otherwise known as Joseph Waterhouse seems to have been Henry's uncle.

Crewmen John Palmer and Christopher Palmer were additionally connected to the Army Chief of Staff, His Royal Highness, Prince Alfred, Duke of Cumberland as their family slipped from King Charles II and his paramour, Barbara Villiers, Duchess of Cleveland.

Missing from the image was Alexander Riley. Riley was Sydney shipper Robert Campbell's brother by marriage and a cousin of Viscount Wentworth In any case the Raby line Riley's mom's last name by birth was Raby. Riley was not in Sydney when the insubordination occurred. However, throughout the following not many years he was conceded broad lots of land. The region from Wooloomooloo through Surry Hills to Zetland was essential for it. Riley Street, which connects these regions today, recognizes Alexander Riley.

The NSW Land Titles Office land move records uncover the exchanges of Riley's territories. Those titles went through a chain of individuals like Viscount Thurlow, Edward Riley and a "C.Barney" through to John Tooth (extraordinary amazing child of King George 111 through an individual accepted to have been Nathaniel Lucas' sister Fanny, a fancy woman of King George IV (Kameruka), John Lucas (Nathaniel Lucas' child (Gundaroo) and......Queen Victoria, Prince Albert's little girl (Gundagai). William Waterhouse, the sibling of first fleeter, Henry Waterhouse, additionally got a square of land in the chain. This square arrived at Sir Joseph Banks (Raby). Lord William IV's child William Montague Clarence Campbell relocated to Australia and settled close to Kameruka and served there as the nearby teacher. His mom was Lady Mary Campbell, girl of the Duke of Argyle, a second cousin of Alexander Riley.

Henry Waterhouse, it just so happens, likewise shipped sheep on his boats. It was he, not John Macarthur, who began the merino sheep industry in Australia. The individual behind the advancement of the merino variety of sheep was.....King George 111.

Henry Waterhouse had the first award where Mr. Robert Campbell set up his stores at The Rocks. While the New South Wales Corps was occupied with the rum traffic, the Royal Naval Officers were involved rather unobtrusively in the wine traffic exchange. Henry had a grape plantation at Parramatta. Phillip Gidley King really set up for the British Government to despatch four French Prisoners of War to Sydney to deal with the juvenile wine industry. Cleverly, it a work to undermine the British, the French Prisoners offered the administrations of four incompetents. On appearance in Sydney, the four were found to have had no openness to the wine making industry. Henry Waterhouse captained a few boats during his vocation however strangely they all definitely visited Sydney routinely. Why? It is noticed that neither Governor Phillip Gidley King nor Governor Bligh acted against the Royal Navy's syndication over the province's wine exchange. It is additionally noticed that the British Navy worked with the lager business with the transportation of the main jumps brings into Australia on board HMS Daedalus in 1805. These bounces were given to a previous mariner, James Squire, for whom a bottling works was subsequently developed in Ryde under the power of Governor King. Lead representative William Bligh recharged the rent. Was this the expert the Army had against King and Bligh?

James Squire was the hawkish for the situation made against Irish renegade Michael Dwyer that prompted the questionable court military choice which upset Bligh and encouraged the rum disobedience. Bligh and Squire were likewise great mates. It will be seen that the candidates to sack Bligh came from all aspects of the state with the special case just of Kissing Point, where Squire resided. There is no question that lager was a basic issue in accelerating the emergency prompting the "Rum Rebellion". Wine might have been too.

John Tooth, grandson of King George IV, procured the previous Squire bottling works. Lead representative King kicked the bucket in England soon after the Rum Rebellion. He was covered in Surrey close to the previous home of convict Nathaniel Lucas with whom he obviously had a decent relationship, and close to the Surrey home of Lord Peter King, the main beneficiary of Viscount Wentworth. There were two Lord Kings. The other, John King, lived in Launceston, Cornwall, origination of Phillip Gidley King.   Nathaniel
Lucas' family's property manager in Thames Ditton, Surrey, was Lord King.

When James Squire's bequest was cut up, John Tooth additionally gathered one of Squire's twelve squares of land. Three different squares of Squire's property passed to a family named Gascoigne from Little Horborough, Buckinghamshire. That town was the site of "Alborough" the home of Viscount Wentworth. In 1888, clearly in recognition of the centennial of European settlement, a young lady brought into the world on Squire's previous domain, was name Olive Gascoigne. Olive Gascoigne was likewise the name of Nathaniel Lucas' first armada spouse ("Lady Penrhyn"). First Fleeter, Olivia (Olive) Gascoigne's child, John Lucas, had hitched Squire's little girl. John Lucas is the one who gained "Gundaroo" through the Riley domains (cousin of Viscount Wentworthand the Duke of Argyle).

When Queen Victoria's child, the Duke of Edinburg, visited Australia, he had just a large portion of a day away from work to himself secretly. Where was he? He was in a pub in Burwood having a quiet ale with Nathaniel Lucas and Olive Gascoigne's grandson, William Lucas, who then owned "Gundaroo" and the Burwood pub. William Lucas' maternal granddad was Captain John Rowley once of the New South Wales Corps. Commander Rowley was the neighborhood specialist for

Captain Henry Waterhouse RN. The Burwood property was initially Rowley's while Burwood was the name of Rowley's origin in Cornwall, close to Launceston, origination of previous Governor Philip Gidley King.

The licensed genius of the "Rum Rebellion" was Captain John McArthur (as he marked his name). That is trash! MacArthur was for some time released from the Army and as an appeal of unwaveringness towards Bligh endorsed in 1806 by numerous individuals of similar pilgrims who denounced Bligh in 1808 uncovers, McArthur was by and large despised by his peers.

The idea that McArthur remained on a city intersection and had the "passing traffic" sign the report requiring Bligh's capture is ludicrous. Individuals who marked the request came from everywhere the province. They either came to town particularly that day or somebody went out to see them to assemble their signatures.

There were 160 people who marked the two petitions to sack Bligh and to say thanks to Major George Johnston for his activity. While applying twelve foundation tests to these men it will be observed that their profiles are not copied. The tests were: District, Emancipist, Free, Army, If Irish, Blue Collar, If Irish, Lace Curtain, Trade or Business, Religion, If English, Class, Civil Servant, Privately utilized, Ship of arrival,

When consolidating all the above highlights, there were no copies. Accordingly, as these candidates were all select by their own doing, the tests demonstrate that those involved were probably going to have been the heads of their individual groups.

The tests went on further. The candidates were verified whether they were hitched or living with somebody. Sixty of them were hitched or had been joined forces. The spouses and young lady companions were then recorded and similar tests were applied. They had a lot in common.

Bingo! There were sixteen first fleeters among the sixty associations. Fifteen accomplices were from the "Woman Penrhyn". There were onlytwenty enduring first armada females in Sydney that day. Esther Abraham's sweetheart, Major George Johnston, officially completed the capture of Bligh and as the appeal was addressed to him he was unable to sign it. Rachel Watkin's better half had passed on and Mary Parker was an individual from the Kissing Point settlement and Margaret Dowling was from the Hawkesbury settlement, which as once huge mob didn't take an interest in the disobedience. These were the main female first fleeters whose accomplices didn't sign the petitions identifying with Bligh's expulsion. There were just four different ladies among the remainder of the associations who had ventured out to Australia on similar boats. This was a "Slip Rebellion". It is currently certain that the ladies put the men up to opposing Bligh.

Why then were these women involved so much as to prod their husbands into becoming their respective community spokesman (or leader)? Why would they have brought about the rebellion? Why would King George's agents here urge and abet them? There is a very simple answer........land. Governor William Bligh made just four land awards during his entire term in office. He additionally dropped four awards (three of them were first fleeter Nathaniel Lucas'). John McArthur didn't begin the fleece business as he is so frequently authorize. He purchased his first sheep from Henry Waterhouse.

King George 111 was a sharp sheep reproducer. Henry Waterhouse could communicate in Spanish. The Merino breed came from Spain initially, despite the fact that Henry Waterhouse's sheep came from South Africa where their appearance there is unexplained. How did King George get the merino's in any case? Henry Waterhouse was associated with His Majesty. All things considered, the Duke of Cumberland, King George's child, was his god-father and his maritime sponsor.

Oddly, a King George 111 clone, referring to himself Mr."James Smith as" joined a similar first armada transport, "Woman Penrhyn". How did Mr."Smith" become a passenger on the first fleet? How come Midshipman Henry Waterhouse was allowed to bring his South African merino sheep with him on a Royal Navy ship? How come King George's breed of merino sheep just happened to be in Capetown in time for the departure of Henry's ship?

In 1808 there were sheep in the image. Then there was the price of wool. The cost of fleece was at record high in Europe on account of the Napoleonic War. In spite of contentions by market analysts, Australia had as of now sent out an amount of fleece to Europe in 1805. The waters had been tested.

The local people could only see that there were millions of acres of potential sheep grazing lands just sitting there doing absolutely nothing commercially while people longed for a better life for themselves and their children.

This then brings the women into it. The youngsters brought out in the main armada or brought into the world in the state's early stages were grown-ups or approaching adulthood by 1808. No mother truly enjoys having a lot of inactive children of
twenty years old or there abouts staying nearby. These were kids who ought to have been trying to more prominent things throughout everyday life, like a home and a task and afterward a sweetheart, or beau. There was positively no future for them here.

The justification for this predicament was Governor William Bligh. Under Bligh's stewardship Sydney stayed a maritime base holding on to despatch scoundrels and warships to pester the Spanish in Peru and Chile to forestall the exchange of silver to the French Treasury. Ho Hum!

When mum's not happy, then dad's not happy either. Lead representative William Bligh was the foe of the arising Australian family for whom he gave no consideration at all. Each mother could see a future on "them thar slopes" past Sydney. Everything Bligh could see was water among here and South America. The mother's infuriated. The exceptionally following day later the disobedience the grounds were opened up. Sure the spouses of those first armada women got large pieces of Australia yet so did royalty.

The Rum Rebellion was in excess of a contention between the British Naval Governors and the British Military Garrison Australia over control of the rum traffic. It was Army versus Navy, it was social issues versus British security needs, it was rum versus lager and wine and, all the more critically, it was the force of the pilgrim ladies versus the organization of the state.

How in the world could Governor WilliaM Bligh have safeguarded his situation against that large number of challengers and tensions? William Bligh really looked up to four uprisings and uprisings during his vocation as a maritime official. In all actuality he was not by and by the monstrosity portrayed later by American film studio M.G.M. also some later film makers. Uprisings and uprisings were "extremely common" with Royal Navy Captains around then. Bligh was similarly in an ideal situation than a significant number of his partners, some of whom lost their lives in insurrections. William Bligh is popular for his revolts as well as, more significantly, on the grounds that he skilfully endure them.

Today, Australians are recorded for their libertarian dream. The British female convicts got it to Australia the main armada buddy.

<u>BOYS</u>

Many young men showed up with their Regiments. One unit had 150 kid warriors. Kid warriors were selected from age 9 years (7 years for drummers and fifers). Before 1820 there were various privately conceived chaps The principal kid enrolled in Australia was really authorized. He was Royal Marine Lieutenant Alexander Ross. Alexander was nine years old on Commissioning. His dad was a serving Major. Lead representative Arthur Phillip went against the commission. Significant Ross utilized the chance to broaden the family income.

This point has some of the time been censured by antiquarians. Nonetheless, cash and family pay had a lot to do with the enrollment of young men. The British Military and Naval pioneers consistently oozed a solid awareness of certain expectations towards the offspring of servicemen. The design was to let a lot of free from the strain on servicemen going to experience harsh criticism. The most grounded message must be conveyed to the men that if they passed on their thankful country, their companions, loved ones would really focus on their friends and family. The British Army and Navy tried to satisfy that commitment.

The British feeling of valor precluded the enlistment of young ladies. Be that as it may, when the young men were enlisted from administration and ex-administration families the young men were paid and instructed. The mother or gatekeeper could gather cash because of the kid so the family pay would be enhanced. Any young ladies in the family would profit from the additional family pay, pitiful as it might have been.

Inevitably young men were persuaded into the military or marines with the goal that the family could get their hands on his compensation. The compensation was just a pitiful three pence a day yet to numerous families that was the main wellspring of income.

The primary Australian conceived kid select was Drummer Francis Spencer. Francis was brought into the world in Sydney in 1790, the child of the main frontier brewer,

James Squire, a Gypsy convict who had shown up on the "Charlotte" in the principal armada, and Mary Spencer a convict who showed up on the "Woman Penrhyn" in the primary armada. James Squire was a bootlegger who confessed at the Kingston Assizes in 1774 to an outrageous overpricing charge to try not to be hanged. He was condemned to life transportation. It is accepted that Squire picked to serve in the British Army and served in North America. After two years he was home and free. In 1784 he was captured for taking chooks from his neighbor and moved for seven years.

James Squire encouraged the Rum Rebellion when he blamed Irish renegade pioneer Michael Dwyer for taking a few hogsheads of lager while on the way. Dwyer was a severe foe of individual Irish Rebel, Arthur Devlin, who was seeking Squire's girl and Francis Spencer's stepsister Priscilla Squire. Dwyer and a few others were court marshaled. Significant Johnston managed the matter. Dwyer was viewed as not liable and was released. Lead representative William Bligh wrongfully over-governed the decision of the Court Martial and sent Dwyer et all to gaol. Bligh was in fact captured by Johnston for acting "ultra-vires", ie., past his legitimate powers.

Some of the story later then can be gotten from the book "Extraordinary Expectations" by Charles Dickens. The contention between the two convicts in Dickens' book takes after a significant part of the ill will that had existed among Devlin and Dwyer. Arthur Devlin later wedded Priscilla Squire and their little girl, Martha, looked like the person "Estella" in the book. Martha's significant other looked like the person "Pip". Martha's dad in law was .. Charles Dickens, who composed the novel while his child Alfred was pursuing her.

According to a few records endorsed by Major George Johnston, Francis Spencer was fifteen months old when selected into the NSW Corps. The Corps' finance doesn't uncover this. Nonetheless, he appears as a drummer in the finance from his seventh birthday.

According to the exploration by the late Captain ChriS Corcorus (U.S.Army
Retired) who wedded James Squire's incredible extraordinary incredible terrific girl), Captain Prentice Coy's Company from the NSW Corps was advanced to the eleventh Devonshires to battle in Europe during the Napoleonic Wars. Assuming this is the case, this was really whenever Australians first saw dynamic help. Commander Coy's organization records are absent for some period during the presence of the NSW Corps and these are the main records that are absent for the pioneer time regiments. A few young men brought into the world in Australia were in the company.

Francis Spencer was subsequently presented on Devonport, Tasmania in 1803 (preceding settlement). A detachment was set there to guarantee the French of a British presence in Van Diemensland. On his dad's drive he established bounces there in his extra time. The organic product was subsequently shipped off Sydney for examination. The outcomes... well the Tasmanians' actually develop the best jumps in Australia. Francis moved to the 73rd Regiment when Lachlan Macquarie showed up and was released to a full life annuity subsequent to having finished more than 20 years administration. He purchased his release and was subbed by Pte.John Lovely in 1812 (Officers could leave. A private's release cost twenty pounds in addition to a substitute warrior must be recruited).

Francis hitched Jane Mary Smith and had twelve chidren. They worked a pastry shop where St. Phillip's Church, Sydney currently stands. Later he worked a Tavern on a similar site. He was a successful businessman who moved from Sydney to Hobart, then to Launceston and finally to Melbourne where he died in 1854.

It is fascinating to take note of that two young men have really been granted the Victoria Cross. One kid, while serving on a ship in World War 1 uniquely monitored a 5 inch firearm for 24 hours, notwithstanding being fundamentally injured. The remainder of the group had been killed. At the point when the activity stopped, he was found dead, still at his post.

GIRLS

Girls were never enrolled into the pilgrim British Army. A few young ladies, deserted by military work force or stranded by the deficiency of the dad in real life, may have been taken in and protected with the young men from darlings to 14 years old. Assuming that happened then it was without a doubt that a military family elected to really focus on the youngster. There was an ethos all through the entire provincial local area that no neglected youngster would do without a family to really focus on it. The modest number of youngsters in the shelters upholds this. Most youngsters in the shelters were from single parent or desperate families, rather than parentless. The nearby neighbor unavoidably took the kid. Scarcely any kids arrived at the halfway houses. A pursuit of the Sydney Female Orphanage records in the Colonial Secretary's Archives, uncovers that it was financed by gifts bought in by Royal Navy Officers. The Sydney Colony was a Royal Navy obligation until 1810. The Royal Navy Officers were all the while adding to the shelter's administration costs until 1822 at least.

Surviving records obviously show that the British Army and the Royal Navy truly thought often about the youngsters related with their work force. The Marines of the Royal Navy actually enroll kids, particularly those from the families which have served their country in war. In 1988 the Portsmouth Division of the Royal Marines found the structure plans for the gig gave to HMS Sirius of the principal armada. The Marines recreated it. They gave the gig to the City of Sydney to honor the significant pretended by their Division in the establishment of the Australian Colonies on 26th January, 1788.

Accompanying the gift was a photo of the twelve kid marines who were then effectively presenting with the Division at the hour of fruition of the work on the new gig.

The Editor once worked close by a previous "Kid" Soldier of the British Army. His dad was killed in France in World War 1. Promptly after his dad's passing the chap was put being taken care of by the British Army. By 1939 he had finished a lifelong term of administration with the British Army and was pensioned off. He then migrated to Australia. He enrolled in the Australian Army on the episode of World War 11 where he served as

a combat zone undertaker. He got a "Notice in Dispatches" for recuperating an officer's body enduring an onslaught. He guaranteed that he revived many "dead" warriors. He finished a subsequent vocation term with the Australian Regular Australian Army. He was pensioned out a second time at 52 years old years.

<u>SCHOOLS</u>

The British Army had a mindful mentality towards the offspring of administration faculty, war widows, warriors killed in real life or deserted by dynamic servicemen or ex-servicemen. Tutoring was accessible in many regiments to those kids who were qualified for an Army gave education.

The records uncover that from the mid-nineteenth century onwards the schools additionally had preparing capacities. It very well may be expected from this that intrigued troopers were given instruction as well assuming they needed it, notwithstanding military training.

The primary proof of a regimental school was that of the New South Wales Corps on Norfolk Island. This would clarify why so many of the youngsters who lived on Norfolk Island during its first settlement (1788-1814) were proficient, notwithstanding the shortfall of a state funded schooling system.

<u>SERVICEWOMEN</u>

British Army Historians have composed that ladies didn't start to present with the British Army until 1856 when Florence Nightingale raised a gathering of attendants to serve in the Crimean War. This statement is conflicting with the records of the Regiments in Australia a long time before then.

Truth be told ladies had served in the British Army before that, at the

same time, distorting themselves as men. For example, there was Scot, "James" Barry, who served in the British Army all through the Napoleonic Wars and afterward on to the Crimean War. She really rose to
the position of Inspector General of Medical Services. She figured out how to make due to finish her vocation, effectively. Strangely, she and Florence Nightingale didn't get on together.

The records uncover a few ladies on the British Army finance in Australia as far back as 1818. The first was situated in the 48th Regiment as right on time as 1818. Another lady was Mrs Annie Astbury of the twelfth Suffolk Regiment who served in two limits. She was a teacher helping the school ace for which she was paid eighteen pounds each year and she was the unit's Monitress for which she was paid a further four pounds each year. In the later limit she administered the youngsters. The last female to serve in the British Army in Australia was Miss Dowling of the eighteenth Royal Irish Regiment in 1870.

In many cases the teacher was the spouse of the Battalion school ace yet in the 48th Regiment this was not the situation. At the turn of the eighteenth/nineteenth Century, the school ace was a Sergeant. Afterward, the school ace didn't have rank. They were set similarly in the unit's association as the paymaster, specialist and the auxiliary. A portion of these positions were displayed on the tactical finance with a tactical position, however the records are not predictable all through the time. The ladies however were constantly shown by their position.

Some Historians affirm that main the relationships of Officers and senior NCO's were endured by the Army. The lower rank faculty were relied upon to give the military all their steadfastness. Never the less privates and corporals wedded or had connections. The Army acknowledged just six life partners in each organization. From 1800 onwards, at any rate, as a trade-off for victuals and authorization to rest in similar bed as their mate in the garisson huts (the couples were accumulated toward one side of the dormitory where they were permitted to wrap a cover around their bed for protection), the mates were relied upon to prepare the organization suppers, clean the wreck and wash the organization laundry.

This assistance was stretched out later to the endorsed life partners

working for the officials of the regiment too. For the extra assignments these women
were paid. Be that as it may, the extent that the regiments in Australia were impacted, the companions were not generally really paid.

FAMILY RECORDS

There were regimental family records. Records were kept of spouses of troops and there were records likewise kept of births, passings and relationships. Separate records of the families were made for an assortment of purposes.

Surviving family records are held in the Mitchell Library, State Library of New South Wales on miniature film, 1162 and 1303 (at piece 3502)

The Public Records Office in London has genealogical references on 3,000 nineteenth century staff. Lamentably they are documented in sequential request under the original last name of the trooper's wife.

Only the NSW Corps and the 99th Regiment kept up with records of a Chaplain. However, it is most likely that almost all regiments had a Chaplain. Ministers records have endure yet these are not accessible in Australia. While there were Church of England Chaplains joined to a regiment, there was no notice of Chaplains of different beliefs while the British Army was in Australia. The Chaplain's Records of the NSW Corps are not held in St.Catherine's House with the other Army Chaplain records. Their current whereabouts are obscure. The 99th Regiments register of its occasions celebrated in Australia are held in St.Catherine's House.

No regimental compensation record in Australia alludes to an Army Chaplain Notwithstanding Chaplains were there. However, there were Chaplains who were neighborhood church with obligations stretched out to cover nearby military unit. It appears to be that the British Government made a considerable gift to the Church of England routinely and consequently the Church of England gave non authorized Chaplain administrations to the military, naval force, police powers, penitentiaries, mental foundations, halfway houses, asylums and little pilgrim stations for the most part, where Chaplains were not on the military establishment.

Official records show that Chaplains were dispatched and had the status rank and the compensation of Major. In its order there was a Chaplains Corps.

During the Macquarie era there was an effort by troops from the 48th Regiment, which was comprised predominantly of Irish (85% Catholic), to secure the appointment of a Catholic Chaplain. It is not known if this was successful nor when Catholic, Jewish, Wesleyan, Methodist or Congregationalist Chaplains etc. were first appointed. The only concession to the Catholic troops known was the approval granted to the Catholic Church to appoint Catholic Priests to the colony, which had been prohibited before that pressure.

Records of the regimental families exist yet these are dissipated and in this undertaking just two were found. The main Marine's family records have made due and they are widely referred to in many works. The 2/eighteenth Regimental records show 92 spouses and notice their given names. This covers 10% of the strength of the regiment at that point. The number and sex of the kids in every family is displayed just as their ages. There were 421 kids, including 205 young men and 216 young ladies. Working out on a favorable to rata premise there were most likely 3,000 spouses and 14,000 kids among the British Army. Most likely a larger part of the youngsters remained in Australia.

The rundowns in this works were haphazardly checked against the files to the Regimental Chaplain's Registers held in St.Catherine's House in London. An examination was made and they were not the equivalent. Just a modest bunch of occasions were found. In the 99th Regiment's register, just Church of England disciples were found. Records of different religions were found here in Australia in the area registers close the regimental barracks.

Some family and friends of men of all ranks can be identified from the payrolls. Numerous men chose for dispatch their compensation on to them. The trooper who did this is distinguished as is the family member or companions to whom he alloted cash from his compensation. Examination of large numbers of these records leads to

the idea that the fighters for the most part sent the cash on to fathers or moms, spouses or sweethearts.

ETHNICITY AND CULTURE

The Editor has distributed chips away at the nationality of the Convicts where 1,600 people with non-British or Celtic identities, doctrine, races and societies were identified.

It was impractical to distinguish the nationality of the soldiers from the records in a similar way as the convict work, in any case, the intrigued will observe that by filtering this work, which is a lot more straightforward than going through months taking a gander at endless supply of payrolls and summons, they could choose the names of individuals which have all the earmarks of being non-British or Celtic.

The impression made by the Editor who checked a couple of individuals recorded on the payrolls is that there were numerous Germans, a few French, Scandanavian, Italian, Lebanese, Portugese and Spanish soldiers. A few Greeks are conceivable. For instance, the family name George might be that of a Greek. The Greek Community know that there were early Greek appearances in Australia, on account of a neighborhood demand made in around 1798 for help to give a Church and a Priest in New South Wales, however they have not yet emphatically distinguished the early Greeks. There were no less than two Americans warriors, one of whom was a Negro.

The Irish were very conspicuous among the soldiers and without a doubt the 48th and eighteenth Regiments seem to have had a larger part Irish representation.

UNIT NUMBERING

From 1870 the British Army Infantry was coordinated into regiments included four legions. Two contingents were extremely durable forces while the other two were state army units. The payrolls of the British Army in Australia, which was only ready before that redesign, uncover something like three unmistakable Battalions joined to each Regiment, numbered 1 or 2 or Reserve. To the extent the records show these were all long-lasting units. The forces are displayed in this work with the legion number going before their individual regiment of the line number. The records additionally allude infrequently to Battalion, now and then number, some of the time not numbered, called the Depot Battalion accepting components of every brigade staying at the Regimental Headquarters in England.

While the 1/twelfth Suffolk Battalion was positioned in Australia, its save Battalion was serving in the Cape of Good Hope settlement. Its subsequent Battalion was in England.

Some individuals from the Depot Battalion were likewise individuals from one of both of the numbered or hold Battalions and all soldiers are displayed on either finance yet cross referred to the Depot Battalion. A portion of the Depot Battalion Troops are remembered for this work. It turned out to be so hard to perceive whether or not they ought to be in the work, as many soldiers were pivoted. A beware of one Battalion's Depot Troops showed that all men had served in Australia eventually during the presence of the unit in Australia.

Notwithstanding the individuals from the Depot Battalion there were various soldiers who stayed in Europe however who were as yet recorded on the posted Battalion's finance. Again a keep an eye on a specific Battalion's rundowns showed that all served in Australia sooner or later. These individuals were dissipated all through the British Isles in upwards of ten areas. The vast majority of them were individuals from the selecting groups.

Two Battalions served twice in Australia. None of the work force serving in Australia on each posting were something similar. To recognize the soldiers serving on each visit, the sign (- 1) or (- 2) is shown later their Regimental Number.

AUSTRALIAN COLONIAL ARMY UNITS

There were a few military units which were only Australian during the early frontier days. These were included staff brought up in Australia for Australian purposes. The first of these was the Loyal Association. While a few of these units are referenced there was essentially just one of them. It was the different Headquarters that changed ownership of the unit. The Loyal Association existed somewhere in the range of 1788 and 1813, that is as per the Dixon Library records. In any case, there were a few references enduring which showed that the Loyal Association existed for significantly longer than that. The records on one part was found in the Parramatta "Argus" documents and he was not brought into the world until 1812.

The Loyal Association was involved mostly of convicts, particularly the individuals who had past military preparing. Part of the reason for the foundation of the province was to given a maritime base to animosity against the Spanish in South America in case of Spain aligning itself with France during battle between Great Britain and France. Plans existed at the beginning of the settlement's establishment for a power to set out from Sydney on at least one of the Royal Navy warships for all time positioned in Sydney from 1788 onwards to pester Spanish vessels, particularly those conveying silver from Lima, Peru. There was a dread that in case of a coalition among France and Spain the silver would arrive at the French Treasury where it would be utilized to fund France's conflict. The unit saw activity in the Castle Hill Exiles' Rebellion in 1804 now and then called "Vinegar Hill", a most shameful reference.

In New South Wales and Tasmania, the first Battalion, 99th Lanarkshire Regiment was the parent unit to a unit of Mounted Police, the harbinger to the Australian Lighthorse. The first 99th Lanarkshires battled in the Maori Wars. This present unit's Mounted Police additionally faced in the Conflict of the Eureka Stockade.

Also in New South Wales and Tasmania, the first Battalion, eleventh Devonshire Regiment was the parent unit of one more separation of Mounted Police. As it turns out, when the 99th Regiment moved, its Mounted Police were isolates to the eleventh Regiment and served independently distinguished however with the eleventh Regiment's Mounted Police.

Some Historians notice that the pioneer legislatures deserted those troopers left behind. Because of an absence of financing, the pioneer legislatures returned to solely chip in powers. To be sure, the New South

Wales Government's tactical financial plan somewhere in the range of 1871 and 1876 was adequate just to pay the wages for a guardian at Victoria Barracks.

Notwithstanding the regiments referenced there were a few units of pioneer volunteers. Their records are dispersed. A few units and their individuals were situated from the records of the NSW Land Titles Office where nearby provincial powers administration is cross referred to awards on release. There is a distributed work on this proof. Some enduring records of the New South Wales pioneer powers to 1908 are held in the New South Wales State Archives.

Between 1798 and 1820 around 200 Australians enrolled into the British Army. Later 1820 there were likely something like this number recruited.

Some Australian enlists later battled in Europe during the Napoleonic Wars, others in Ambon, Dutch East Indies (1828), Ceylon (1815), on the Indian Frontier (different occasions), in the Burma War 1824-25.

VETERAN AND INVALID UNITS

Veteran and Invalid Companies/Battalions were not similar units. Invalid, incidentally, isn't articulated as in the word importance handicapped, viz., "in-va-top". It was articulated "In-val-id", implying that the soldiers concerned had not yet been approved to a position/rank on the approved strength of their parent regiment, yet that they were on that Unit's finance and serving under its Commanding Officer.

This attestation isn't reliable with the perspectives on British Military Historians who notice that the units were involved fighters in poor wellbeing. In any case, the "Invalid" units in Australia were not involved the sick.

The genuine significance of "invalid" was "exaggerated". Invalids in Australia were normally the soldiers abandoned by a withdrawing Regiment who were given the choice of remaining or leaving or they were purposely abandoned. Regardless the British Army didn't generally take the entire regiment on move starting with one country then onto the next.

The regimental base camp and the enrolling and preparing areas stayed appended to the stop in Britain or Ireland. Numerous units had staff disengaged from one side of the planet to the other, particularly in England where they attempted selecting obligations. While many regiments were named after regions, their staff didn't really come from them. In this manner the name of the regiment can't be depended on to recognize a warriors origin. Be that as it may, the enrolling work force's station is referenced on the "Assistants Roll" which is regularly joined to the finance. Their area could lessen the choices of a fighter's probably spot of birth. Regardless some place in the majority of the payrolls later 1810 notice, refered to in the comments segment, was regularly made of the fighters occupation and birth place.

Many soldiers were abandoned on the regiment's takeoff on account of wounds, disorder and family needs. On its landing in the following station the approaching regiment would assume control over those left behind by the assuaged Regiment. Where a regiment surpassed its approved strength when it ingested different soldiers, Invalid Companies were then made by the approaching regiment for finance purposes. Consequently an authoritative and bookkeeping component perceived any overabundance of troops over the endorsed number of troops of each particular position where the present circumstance arose.

The distinction among Veteran and Invalid was that assuming there were troops who were not to be connected to an approaching guardian unit they would be joined to an imaginary Royal Veteran Battalion. It was imaginary in that there was no genuine authoritative order free of the unit to which the men were really serving. It was completely a paper unit intended to pay, pack and proportion the soldiers involved.

There are three separate Veteran units recorded in this work, viz, the fourth and eighth Royal Veteran Battalion and the Royal New South Wales Veterans Corps. A few organizations are likewise mentioned.

As to the actual men, they just wore the separate withdrew regiment's outfits and strutted and filled in as though they were a full individual from the regiment.

Where the Royal Veteran Battalions were concerned, the parent regiment can't forever be speculated. This was particularly the situation with the fourth Battalion. Once in a while two regiments or more were positioned in a similar province at the same time and in this way one can't expect which regiment went about as the parent unit. On account of the eighth Battalion, all the staff concerned were consumed into the 102nd Regiment of Foot and can be obviously situated on its finance. The fourth Battalion was recorded on one finance marshal for the 102nd however they didn't stay posted there.

The Invalid and Veteran Companies would post the posts of the leaving Regiment assuming that there was a hole between the takeoff and appearance of the changing Regiments.

BORDER POLICE

In actuality the Border Police was important for a line Regiment. Albeit a composite, ie., compromised of staff collected from a wide scope of units, it was shaped to secure Australia's northern region working in remote spots in 1838.

Soldiers were not enlisted into this unit, they were condemned into it. Weaklings from the Regiments of the British Army in India were moved into it on their recuperation, then, at that point, delivered out to Australia.

The unit was joined to a regiment positioned in Australia as though it were one of its organizations. Nonetheless, it was given a messy job.

Very little exposure is given to the Aborigine Border War in Queensland. It persevered for some years.

Starvation pushed a considerable lot of the Aborigines inland. Nonetheless, there came when that was not the situation. This was the point at which the outskirts, or line as local people called it, moved inland. The Aborigines lived off the land and there was adequate food assets for them. So the Aborigines retaliated. An Aborigine could ship off six lances in the time a fighter could reload his rifle.

First the infringing pilgrims needed to safeguard themselves. Then, at that point, came the police troopers and afterward at last the British Army. The unit included was known as the Border Police.

Regrettably, the staff records of this unit were not located.

MILITARY PENSIONER UNIT

There was such a unit alluded to as the Military Pensioners which serverd in Eastrn Australia. It is unquestionably referenced to scholarly references. It isn't sure however now that it is a similar unit alluded to as the Royal New South Wales Veterans Company. Assuming it isn't a similar then no work force records were found. Such a unit was 4especially brought for administration up in Western Australia.

The Vandiemenian Police unit which served in the Eureka mobs of 1854 was framed from among the military pensioners.

VANDIEMENIAN CONVICT POLICE

Despite scholarly reference and Television programs portraying Vandiemenian convict police presenting with the Port Phillip District (Victoria) Police Force in 1854, this is a fallacy.

There may have been convicts ammong these individuals however the Vandiemenian Police was truth be told a line regiment of the British Army.

Able bodied military beneficiaries were Army Reservists. The British Army called up all tactical retired people in Tasmania (Vandiemensland). Some might have been taken from Port Arthur Penitentiary. That is debatable.

The unit was shipped off Ballarat to help the nearby police with the unsettling influences on the goldfields. War Office list in the Dixon Library, State Library of New South Wales (at 2.2) are illuminating on this matter.

NEW SOUTH WALES CORPS AND THE 102ND REGIMENT OF FOOT

It is by and large affirmed that the New South Wales Corps turned into the 102nd Regiment of Foot (later the 100th Royal Dublin Fusiliers). History specialists regularly notice that Colonel Lachlan Macquarie showed up with his own Regiment, the 73rd Regiment, and disbanded the "Rum Corps. This is totally wrong.

Lachlan Macquarie was not the Commander of the 73rd Regiment. Rather, Colonel George Harris was the Commander. The first Battalion of the 73rd was only moved to Australia on a turn premise as the 102nd Regiment was expected for return to England and the NSW Corps, which was not a line regiment of the British Army (it was a specific reason unit controlled by the Army for the Secretary for Colonies), was to be disbanded. Macquarie was the Officer Commanding the first Battalion of the Regiment and a subordinate to Colonel Harris.

Having gone through a few redesigns somewhere in the range of 1808 and 1810, the New South Wales Corps of 26th January, 1808 (the day Bligh was captured) looked similar to the 102nd Regiment of Foot in late 1809 (later the Rum Rebellion and before Macquarie's arrival).

Over 140 soldiers of the 102nd Regiment had been moved from England between 26th January, 1808 and tenth January, 1810. North of twenty of the Corps had kicked the bucket meanwhile while 70 of its positions had been discharged.

Prior to its takeoff from England for Australia, Lt. Colonel John Harris (no connection of George) had shown up to rearrange the 102nd Regiment of Foot. The rearranged Regiment included just three Officers and five Sergeants of the previous New South Wales Corps. The Officers were Major William Patterson, Captain Hugh Piper and Lt. William Minchin. Colonel Harris rearranged the 102nd Regiment into a 400 and 73 man unit involving 300 and 47 soldiers currently on foundation. Nonetheless, of those soldiers, twelve sergeants and 100 Privates, previously of the NSW Corps were put into an Invalid Company. This is the "unit" by and large alluded to as the "Invalid Company" of the time. That Company stayed in Australia later the 102nd Departed. Truth be told 265 soldiers of the Rum Corps stayed later the 102nd left for England.

About 100 privates of the 102nd Regiment were moved to the 73rd

Regiment and the 73rd consumed the 102nd's Invalid Company. There could have been no previous Corps Officers or Sergeants moved to the 73rd Regiment. The equilibrium of the work force, which incorporated the unplaced ex-Rum Corps Officers were presented on the eighth Royal Veteran Battalion, not to the 102nd Regiment.

Major Johnston was shipped off England independently where he was Court-Marshaled for capturing Governor William Bligh. He was viewed as liable, downgraded to private and cashiered. He pursued his conviction and the decision was subsequently toppled. He was reestablished as a Lt. Colonel and he resigned to "Annandale" in Sydney.

When the 102nd Regiment left for England in mid 1810 short of what 100 of its 376 leaving faculty had over year and a half assistance with the unit. There were really a lot more New South Wales Corps staff serving in the 73rd Regiment than there were staying in the leaving 102nd Regiment. Thusly, there was just a little association between the men of the Rum Corps and the withdrawing 102nd Regiment of Foot. Unexpectedly a further 10 Rum Corps veterans

kicked the bucket on the way back to England. These incorporated the units previous Adjutant, Major William Patterson. This was a man that notwithstanding the underhanded standing that endure the takeoff of the NSW Corps gave a lot to Australia in its early stages. The Patterson River north of Maitland in New South Wales commendably recognizes him. He is especially reviewed for keeping up with steadiness in the settlement later Governor Bligh was eliminated. He was not a member in the disobedience but rather when he became mindful of it he would not assist Bligh with reestablishing him to Governor. Properly so!

The 102nd Regiment was renamed the 100th Regiment in 1815 however the unit strength by then was just 224, of whom just 51 had served in Australia.

3RD MARINES

The Third Marines was a company of work force presented on Fort Essington in Northern Australia 1848-49. The subtleties of these work force were not located.

<u>fourth MARINES</u>

The Fourth Marines is a slippery gathering. The presence of this impromptu gathering was just recognized from the card lists in the Dixon Library, State Library of New South Wales and the State Archives of Tasmania. Early local almanacs and Directories such as the Sands Sydney Directory mention them in Sydney and Hobart.

The presence of Marine Officers was first recognized in Hobart-based references for the 1830s and 1840s. Marine Captain John Morgan was all around reported, even down to the house where he resided. Enquiries made with Naval Historians uncovered that there were Marines positioned at Garden Island, Sydney, until 1911.

Royal Navy staff might in any case be positioned in Australia. The Editor was
once utilized in a position where he liaised with the Royal Navy Office in Sydney. This was situated in HMAS "Penguin" in Balmoral. The Royal Navy gave the Sydney Port Naval Operations Superintendent, to some extent up to the last part of the 1970s, and the Australian Navy's Nuclear War Defense Officer.

<u>ROYAL MARINES LIGHT INFANTRY</u>

The Royal Marines Light Infantry was a unit of nearly twenty faculty sent by the British Government to post an establishment at Somerset on the Cape York Peninsular and Ford Dundas in Northern Australia in 1865.

No work force records for this unit were located.

<u>BRITISH BENGAL ARMY</u>

Between 1820 and 1830 there was an Artillery and Infantry separation of the British Bengal Army in Australia. Hints of its essence were distinguished in Western Australia when a party of advanced wayfarers found the remaining parts of a Catholic sort cavern around 400 miles inland from the Northern Western Australian Coast. It has been assessed to be around 400 years of age. Its reality was distributed in a Yorkshire paper in 1830 which was too soon for any of the British Army in Australia endeavors. The view taken at the time was that the unit that found the site was from India. Such a unit is recorded however just three of its faculty were distinguished. They were Captain Campbell, Bengal Army Artillery (1828 Census), Major James Stewart and Boxo Khan, Bengal Army Infantry (1822 Muster).

BOMBAY MARINE

A unit recorded as the "Bombay Marine" showed up in Sydney on board the "Tracker" in 1817. This was a unit of the British East India Company's

Colonial Indian Navy. There are a few books on this unit that has arisen later as the Indian Navy. It was transformed while in Australia as the eleventh Bombay Native Infantry. Further neighborhood subtleties were not found.

STATISTICS

(* Estmate as it were. Individual names not found)

UNIT PERSONNEL

second Company, sixth Battalion, Royal Artillery (2C6B) 53

sixth/tenth Battalion, Royal Artillery (6-10B) 27

eighth Company, tenth Battalion, Royal Artillery (8C10B)

32 first Battery, first Brigade, Royal Artillery (1B1B) 110

seventh Battery, second Brigade, Royal Artillery

(7B2B) 109 first Battery, fifteenth Brigade, Royal

Artillery (1B15B) 144

first Marines (New South Wales and Norfolk Island) (1M) 264

second Marines (Port Phillip (Melbourne and Van Diemensland) (2M)

60 third Marines (Fort Essington) (3M)* 20

fourth Marines (Sydney and Hobart) (4M) 1

Royal Marines Light Infantry (Cape York)* 20

Border Police (BP)* 120

1/third East Kent (The Buffs) Regiment of Foot (3) 766

1/fourth Kings Own Regiment of Foot (4) 1320

1/fifth Northumberland Regiment of Foot (5) 1

1/eleventh North Devonshire Regiment of Foot (11)

2368 1/twelfth East Suffolk Regiment of Foot (12)

1540

1/fourteenth West Yorkshire (Prince of Wales Own) Regiment of Foot (14) 1057

1/seventeenth Leicestershire Regiment of Foot (17) 1052

1/eighteenth Royal Irish Regiment of Foot

(18) 887 1/21st Royal North British Fusiliers

(21) 880 1/22nd Cheshire Regiment of Foot

(22) 1 1/24th Warwick Regiment of Foot (24)

1 1/25th Kings Own Borderers (25) 1

1/28th North Gloucestershire Regiment of Foot (28) 1393

1/29th Regiment of Foot (29) 1

1/33rd Duke of Wellingtons Regiment of Foot (33) 2

1/34th Cumberland Regiment of Foot (34) 1

1/39th Dorsetshire Regiment of Foot (39) 935

2/40th Somersetshire (first visit) Regiment of Foot (40-1) 1010

2/40th Somersetshire (second visit) Regiment of Foot (40-2) 1678

1/41st Welsh Regiment of Foot 1

1/43rd Monmonthshire 1

1/45th Regiment of Foot (45) 1

1/46th South Devon Regiment of Foot (46) 778

1/47th Lancashire Regiment of Foot (47) 1

1/48th Northhamptonshire Regiment of Foot (48) 1572 1/50th

West Kent (first visit) Regiment of Foot (50-1) 899 1/50th West

Kent (second visit) Regiment of Foot (50-2) 555

2/51st Yorkshire West Riding Light Infantry Regiment of Foot (51) 1540 1/57

West Middlesex Regiment of Foot (57) 990

1/58th Rutlandshire Regiment of Foot (58) 1207 1/61st

South Gloucestershire Regiment of Foot (61) 1 1/62nd

Wiltshire Regiment of Foot 1

1/63rd West Suffolk Regiment of Foot (63) 1032

2/65th Yorkshire North Riding Regiment of Foot (65) 957 1/68th

Durham Regiment of Foot (68) 1

1/70th Surry Regiment of Foot (68) 1

1/73rd Royal Highlanders Regiment of Foot (1/73) 1233

2/73rd Royal Highlanders Regiment of Foot (2/73) 82 73rd

Invalid Regiment of Foot (INV) 103

1/74th Assaye Regiment of Foot 1

1/77th East Middlesex Regiment of Foot (77) 918

1/80th Staffordshire Volunteers Regiment of Foot (80) 1043

1/91st Argyleshire Highlanders (91) 1

1/96 Manchester Regiment of Foot (96) 1493 1/99th

Lanarkshires Regiment of Foot (99) 2014 1/102nd

Regiment of Foot (102) 245

102nd Invalid Regiment of Foot (INV) 103 Ceylon

Rifle Regiment 1

Military Pensioners Detachment (MPD)* 20

eleventh Mounted Police (11MP) 132

eleventh New South Wales Military Mounted Police (11NSWMMP)* 15

21st Mounted Police (under their connected unit)

51st Mounted Police (51MP) 4

57th Mounted Police (under their appended unit) 80th

Mounted Police (80MP) 69

99th Mounted Police (99MP) 123

Boys (under their joined units)

Command Headquarters (HQ) 8

Chaplains (under their appended unit...misc. payment folio) Loyal

Association (local army type unit not included)

New South Wales Corps (NSWC) 1062

Odd Bods (under their appended unit)

Parramatta Loyal Association (civilian army type unit excluded)

Royal Artillery (not in any case under their joined unit) (RA) 7

Royal Engineers (RE) 102

twentieth Royal Sappers and Miners (Western Australia) (20RSM)* 65

Royal Sappers and Miners (South Australia) (RSM) 5

Royal Hospital (RH) 17

Royal Staff Corps (RSC) 142

Royal Survey (RS) 2

Royal New South Wales Veterans Corp (RNV) 55

Schools (under their connected unit)

Servicewomen (under their joined unit)

Surgeons (under their joined unit...infantry just)

first Veterans Company Regiment of Foot (1VC) 102

second Veterans Company Regiment of Foot (2VC)

1

second Royal Veterans Battalion Regiment of Foot (2VB)

56 fourth Royal Veterans Battalion Regiment of Foot

(4VB) 118 eighth Veterans Battalions Regiment of Foot

(8VB) 28

Veterinarians (under their connected unit...(Military Train and Artillery just)

Military Train (WT) (see under their appended unit)

HMS "Fantome" gunners detached to 12th Suffolk Regiment*

HMS "Electra" gunners detached to 12th Suffolk Regiment*

Port Phillip Mounted Police detachment to 12th Suffolk Regiment

Port Phillip District Police detachment to 12th Suffolk Regiment

TOTALS 34,809

The absolute number of faculty distinguished in this work is 34,139. The leftover staff couldn't be identified.

<u>BIBLIOGRAPHY</u>

<u>A.BOOKS</u>

Baxter, C.J., 1822 Muster Australian Biographical and Generalogical Record, Sydney 1996

Cobley, J., Sydney Cove, 1788-1800, Vols 1-5, Angus and Robertson, 1962

Crowley, F. (ed.), A New History of Australia, Heinemann, Melbourne, 1976

DonoHoe, J.H., The Catholics Of New South Wales 1788-1820 And Their Families, NSW State Archives Authority, Sydney, 1988

DonoHoe, J.H., Convicts And Exiles Transported From Ireland 1790-1820, Donohoe, Sydney, 1989

DonoHoe, J.H., The Forgotten Australians The Non-Anglo or Celtic Convicts and Exiles, , Donohoe, Sydney, 1991

DonoHoe, J.H., Norfolk Island 1788-1813 The People And Their Families, Donohoe, Sydney, 1986

DonoHoe, J.H., Tasmania 1803-1820 The People And Their Families, Donohoe, Sydney, 1988

DonoHoe, J.H., Mary, Mary Breen Where Are You, Minerva Press, London, 1995

DonoHoe, J.H., The British Army in Australia 1788-1870 Index of Personel, Sydney, 1997

DonoHoe, J.H., Treat, JS Shaw North Publishing, Sydney 2011

Erickson, R., The Brand On His Coat, UNA Press, Canberra, 1983

Erickson, R.(ed.), The Dictionary of Western Australia, University of Western Australia, Perth, 1979

Fowler, S, Army Records For Family Historians, Public Records Office, London, 1992

Gillen, M., The Founders of Australia, Library of Australian History, Sydney, 1989

<u>Historical Records of Australia, Commonwealth Government Printer,</u>

Melbourne, 1914

Historical Records of New South Wales, New South Wales Government Printer, Sydney, Various Years

Johnson, K. and Sainty, M. (eds.), 1828 Census (of New South Wales), Library of Australian History, Sydney, 1977

McNicoll, R.R., The Royal Australian Engineers, Royal Australian Engineers corps Committee, Canberra, 1977

Oakley, G., Our Military AnceStors, J.S.Battye Library, Perth, 1991.

Pike, D. (ed.), Australian Dictionary of Biography, 1788-185O, Volumes 1-2, Melbourne University Press, 1966

Rubinstein, W.D., The Jews in Australia, AE Press, Melbourne, 1986

Seaton,R., The Deserters, Adelaide 1983

Stanley, P., The Remote Garrison: The British Army in Australia 1788-1870, Kangaroo Press, Kenthurst, 1986

Stephen, L. and Lee, S. (ed's.), The Dictionary of National Biography, Oxford University Press, Oxford, 1973

Tipping, M., Convicts Unbound The Story of the Calcutta Convicts and Their Settlement in Australia, Viking O'Neil, Melbourne, 1988

Ward, R., Australia A Short History, Ure Smith, Sydney, 1975

Ward, R., The Australian Legend, Oxford University Press, Melbourne, 1974

WaTts, M.J. and C.T., My Ancestor Was In The British Army, Society of Genealogists, London, 1995

B. PERIODICALS

Telegraph, Daily Telegraph, Sun-Herald and Daily Mirror.

C. PAPERS

DIXON LIBRARY, STATE LIBRARY OF NEW SOUTH WALES

Victoria Lt.Governor's papers and Reports of the British Army into the Eureka occurrence. A2434